"When the situation gets worse in proportion to the effort made to correct the problem, this is a signal that the methods being employed are probably part of the problem."

Carl E Ockert

Compassion AND COMMON SENSE

Carl E. Ockert

Library of Congress Catalog Card Number 79-92791

ISBN 0-9603926-1-0 (Paperbound)
ISBN 0-9603926-0-2 (Clothbound)

Published by
MCP Books
P.O. Box 273
Germantown, Md.
20767
Printed in the United States of America

DEDICATION

To God from Whom, directly or indirectly, comes every good gift.

To George D. Stoddard, President of the University of Illinois, who showed me the moral imperative, "If we can't, who can?".

To Leonard E. Read, President of the Foundation for Economic Education, who taught me the theory of freedom.

To the Congressional Staff, who taught me the facts of politics.

To the Engineers at the Knolls Atomic Power Laboratory, who listened.

CONTENTS

Introduction

"For He maketh His sun to rise on the evil and on the good, and sendeth rain on the just and on the unjust."
(Matt. 5:45)

Our religious heritage teaches us compassion. Every seeker of high public office must convince the voters that he is concerned about them, whether in fact he is or not. A leader who has a program that would solve some important social problem will often lose out to his opponent who has no solution but really shows his concern.

On the other hand, practical politicians know that in order to get elected, they will need huge sums of money to finance their campaigns, and to get this money they must satisfy the special interests that contribute to their campaign funds. The resulting conflict of interest between their expressed concern about social problems, and their unpublicized commitments to special interests makes most politicians skilled hypocrites. It can also prevent honest men from ever trying to seek public office.

Therefore, if social problems are ever going to be solved, the solutions must come from the people themselves. We cannot wait for our elected experts to come up with the answers. Furthermore, any solution must not only be able to solve the problem technically, it must also be consistent with the basic public demand for compassion and fair play.

The free market, for example, is the most efficient solution to most economic problems. But there is no compassion in the free market. The rewards go to the competent, the incompetent can starve if they cannot compete. This harsh reality turns many away from the free market, and they try to find compassionate solutions to problems by some form of socialism. But socialism doesn't work very well, and socialistic solutions breed more problems than they solve. Some of our worst problems such as inflation and unemployment are largely the result of our attempts to solve other problems by such methods.

Our objective should be to first understand the realities of the problem, then find the most efficient way to solve the problem, and then make whatever changes that are necessary to meet our criteria for compassionate fair play.

Common sense tells us that human nature does not change, and so any solution that requires general human nature to change is doomed to fail. Therefore an effective solution must go along with, rather than against, our basic human nature. This also means that we cannot expect perfect solutions to any problem. We must learn toleration for some remaining degree of evil and injustice, even after the basic problem has been solved. Freedom is not possible if we insist on forcing everyone to do right as we see it.

When effective solutions are applied, social problems disappear. Therefore, when problems persist, the most likely reason is that the "solutions" are making the problem worse. In trying to find an effective solution, our first step should be to see what would happen if we did the opposite of what was previously thought to be the right solution.

Our common sense tells us that the referee should not be one of the ball players. Similarly if our government is to act as our economic referee, it should not be competing with private enterprise. We also know that too many rule changes spoil the game. Our laws should be written so that they automatically adjust to changing conditions, rather than having a board of bureaucrats issuing new rules all the time. Perhaps this could be done if some of our laws were patterned to simulate the automatic self balancing actions of the free market.

Our common sense also tells us that value is determined by utility and desire, and that prices should be determined by competition. We should not allow Marxist concepts to pervert our laws by defining value as labor cost, or price as a government responsibility. We know by bitter experience that whenever the government fixes prices, it produces either shortages or surpluses depending on whether the price is set lower or higher than the free market price.

Our compassion tells us that consumers should be protected against ineffective products. But our common sense tells us that government bureaucrats have no infallible means for deciding what is effective and what is not. Therefore we should take judicious action to make sure that consumers are provided with a full disclosure of relevant information, but knowledgeable consumers should not be protected against themselves, or prevented from obtaining products they desire just because their judgment differs from that of the Bureaucracy.

This book is unlike most books on social problems in that specific proposals are offered. Most books analyze problems but are careful not to suggest any specific solutions. It is easy to get agreement as long as what is being proposed is not specific. But non-specific proposals do not solve problems. Therefore every proposal in this book is specific enough to be evaluated as to whether it is likely to succeed or fail. Since our experience is that most new ideas are impractical, it is unlikely that all of these proposals will find universal acceptance. But if even one finds sufficient acceptance to be given a fair trial, all of the effort that has gone into the preparation of this book will not have been in vain.

I

UNEMPLOYMENT

Why Unemployment?

We have the persisting problem of unemployment because there is widespread confusion as to its real causes. The few economists who understand these causes are continually contradicted by the many who do not. Since the economists contradict each other, it is no wonder that the politicians and the press can say anything they wish without embarrassment, since no one can tell whether they are talking sense or nonsense. Therefore the first step that is needed to solve the unemployment problem is for the people to understand the real causes. Once the real causes are understood, the solutions become obvious.

One of these causes comes from the confusion over the question of voluntary and involuntary unemployment. Is there any real difference between the case where a man refuses to work and the case where he is willing to work but cannot find a job?

If a man is happily employed at a good job, and is suddenly laid off, with no other job available that pays as well, he may argue that his unemployment is involuntary. Indeed it is, with respect to the particular job he has lost. But it is voluntary with respect to other jobs which are available. If the best alternative job pays only half as much, his decision not to work may be understandable, but it really means that he prefers unemployment rather than that particular job.

Unemployment would never occur if we could all define our jobs to suit our individual desires relative to work content, working conditions, interest, power, importance, pay, etc. As long as we focus on the job that was lost, or the job that is desired but not available, we can talk about "involuntary" unemployment. But if we are to work, we must accept some available job, and whether we do or not depends on our evaluation of the costs and benefits resulting from that decision. If the advantages obtained from accepting a particular job outweigh the disadvantages, we choose employment. If not, we choose unemployment. In any case the choice is ours.

Therefore if we want to see people employed, we should recognize that those who are not working will not work until their overall motivations for finding and accepting the best available job become higher than their overall motivations for remaining unemployed. In a later section, we will examine one way in which this can be conveniently accomplished.

Another fallacy that causes unemployment is the idea that minimum wage laws benefit the disadvantaged by raising their income. It is true that some may be benefited because the minimum wage law acts as their bargaining agent. But the main effect is not to raise wages but to eliminate jobs. Many people are handicapped by youth, inexperience, mental and emotional problems, or physical disabilities such that the product of their work is less valuable to an employer than the cost of their minimum wage. The minimum wage laws make the hiring of these people either illegal or unprofitable. Since employers cannot stay in business by losing money, and since they do not like to operate from a jail cell, the end result is that there are no available jobs for these disadvantaged people. They are forced to remain unemployed because our society has made it illegal for them to work! Until we find some satisfactory way to relieve this problem, we will have persisting unemployment among all those who are disadvantaged in their ability to do useful work.

A third area of confusion comes from the inherent conflict between our goal for increasing wealth and our goal of full employment. This conflict arises because the natural result of a general increase in wealth is additional leisure. This is fine when the leisure is properly distributed in terms of more holidays, vacations, and shorter work weeks. But it is not so fine when the leisure is maldistributed such that some are discouraged from working at all so that others may continue working full time.

In a primitive society people tend to work just enough to stay alive, and there is very little accumulation of wealth. Why don't they work harder and accumulate more wealth? There may be other reasons, but the main reason is that it is too much effort, and the satisfactions obtained by possessing more goods does not seem worth the effort needed to obtain them. What is needed is more incentive to work, and this comes from the availability of capital.

Capital can be considered anything that is used to facilitate the production or the acquisition of wealth. It may be tools, or equipment, or education, whatever will assist in the production or acquisition of property. When a society starts to consume less than it produces and to invest the difference into capital goods, it can no longer be considered primitive. It is the capital equipment that allows productivity to increase and wealth to be accumulated.

It would seem that if tools make work easier, it would result in more leisure. After all, the same subsistence can now be obtained with less time and effort. Why not work less? But very often just the opposite occurs. Jobs become available and people choose to work more rather than less!

The reason for this strange choice is that the people are enticed by what appears to be high pay compared to the product of their previous labor without the tools. Without the tools provided by capital, the value of the work is so low that it isn't worth doing more than just enough to stay alive. But with tools, the benefits obtained by working a few more hours appear much greater than the required sacrifice of effort and leisure. So initially, at least, capital formation creates higher pay and a demand for labor that causes many to choose to work longer and harder than they did before.

As production rises, consumption also rises. People discover new needs, develop new desires, and new jobs and industries are created to satisfy these desires. As production continues to rise, it may reach a level that exceeds the combined rate of consumption and capital formation. When this occurs, there is a continuing increase in the general wealth as measured by the inventory of consumer goods owned by the people.

Sooner or later, a rising inventory of goods in the hands of the consumers produces less and less desire for more goods. The economists call this the Law of Diminishing Marginal Utility. It is easy to see that for any particular good, the usefulness and subjective value of each additional unit becomes less and less as more units are acquired. The second pair of shoes is less useful than the first, and the ninth less than the eighth, and so on.

This tendency for any particular good is also true for all goods, since people tend to acquire the particular goods that are most needed and desired first. Thus as property is accumulated, the desire, demand, and the subjective value for any given consumer good decreases. The result is that the real (inflation adjusted) price that people are willing to pay for that good also decreases.

The effect of all this is to cause leisure to reappear. It starts to reappear when the desire for the additional goods being produced diminishes faster than productivity increases. If productivity increases faster, then even though each unit produced has less subjective value, the fact that more are produced with the same effort compensates, and the overall value of the work does not diminish. But when productivity tapers off, or when the marginal utility value falls faster than productivity is increasing, then the overall value of the product of a work hour will diminish and the overall motivation to work will change to favor more leisure. These motivations operate by lowering prices and wages, and by layoffs, production cutbacks, clearance sales, business losses, etc. The end result is a recession in business activity and more leisure for the workers.

In other words, people without goods are willing to work hard for low wages and to pay high prices because of the intensity of their desire for consumer goods. But as their material needs are satisfied, their desire for still more goods diminishes, and there comes a point where they will not pay enough for the products of their work to cover the cost of its production. At that point, the production of goods must then slow down.

This process is entirely natural and inevitable. The reduction in production caused by the accumulation of inventory automatically acts to reduce that inventory, since more is now being consumed than produced. As the inventory of consumer goods decreases, the effect of the Law of Diminishing Marginal Utility reverses and the subjective value of consumer goods starts to rise again. When the consumption of the stored goods has proceeded to the point where the value of the products of work exceeds the cost of production, consumer demand reappears, production picks up, and leisure is again reduced. Thus the natural tendency is to approach an equilibrium level of wealth versus leisure, with some fluctuation of production above and below the level of average consumption.

Since this whole process has the inevitability of

natural law in operation, we should stop kidding ourselves that we can prevent it from happening. On the other hand, once we see that leisure is an unavoidable result of increasing wealth, we will focus our attention on ways for accommodating rather than preventing the natural appearance of increased leisure. Trying to prevent it by artificial stimulation of the economy merely makes the recession worse when it finally comes. Why not accept the leisure, distribute it in shorter work weeks, more vacations, more holidays? Why not enjoy the results of our success?

Capital produces wealth and wealth produces leisure. We have three choices. We can suffer the unemployment, we can distribute and enjoy the leisure, or we can prevent the appearance of leisure by destroying wealth and the capital investment that produces wealth.

At first glance, the proposal to avoid leisure by destroying wealth seems insane. But history shows that of all the methods used to fight unemployment, the method of destroying wealth has been the most effective!

It was the tremendous destruction of World War II that brought us out of the great depression of the 1930's. Since then we have had a succession of wars and arms races, all of which divert employment from creating consumer wealth. In addition, we have created innumerable government agencies which destroy our wealth by endless regulation, red tape, restrictions and confusions which paralyze our productive efficiency and divert millions of work hours to nonproductive tasks.

As if that were not enough, we have given the Federal Reserve the power to print unlimited supplies of money and the resulting inflation has raised havoc with our basic capital investment. In the USA, real capital investment is now almost zero due to the fact that the government will not allow industry to account for the effects of inflation in their depreciation calculations. The government forces businesses to report real losses as profits, by disallowing the increased depreciation that is needed to cover the inflated costs of replacing worn out equipment. Then it taxes these arbitrarily defined "profits" and thereby increases the real losses, which of course are hidden from the stockholders by bank loans which gradually transfer the ownership to the banks. The result in many cases is a general reduction in equity capital, and this would be reflected in an extremely low level for the Dow Jones Averages if they were properly adjusted to reflect the greatly reduced value of the dollar.

Our wealth destroying efforts to prevent the appearance of leisure and the enjoyment of a shorter work week has on the whole been very successful, although it has not eliminated a growing residual level of unemployment. But if we had not so effectively destroyed our wealth, the technological gains in productive efficiency over the last thirty years would have given us a choice between a 20 hour work week, or a 50% unemployment. How nice of our government to destroy our wealth so that we can have more work and less leisure!

It is time to change our approach to the problem of leisure. Let's solve the problem by systems that automatically distribute the leisure when it appears. Let's have programs that will remove the artificial restraints and the misapplied subsidies which concentrate the leisure in the form of unemployment on those who are disadvantaged. Let's share the leisure and enjoy it!

Employment Benefits

Why does a man stay unemployed, especially when there are many jobs available? We can say that if the sum total of incentives which motivate him to get another job are less than those incentives that motivate him to stay unemployed, he will stay unemployed. We can also say that he will continue to be unemployed until there is a change in his overall motivation pattern. Unfortunately, such adverse conditions can occur rather frequently where the worker is really serving his logical best interests by refusing employment. Sometimes it is because he receives more money being unemployed than he would make, after the various deductions, if he were working full time at some particular temporary job. Sometimes it is because he would lose future job security if he took temporary employment.

Suppose someone offered you a tax-free pension of about 75% of your present take-home pay, on the condition that you do not accept "regular" employment. Would you be tempted? Could you not find a do-it-yourself project that would let you earn (or save) the difference in income, and leave plenty of time to enjoy yourself? Think of the books and the music, think of the hunting and fishing, think of the travel and adventure, not to mention liquor, dope, sex, and the fun of picketing people you don't like!

I think a lot of middle class people would be tempted. I would for sure. There are many things that I would like to do which I will never have the time to do. However, the law does not offer me such a deal. Unemployment benefits can be as high as 75% of the take-home pay for a minimum wage worker, but every state has some sort of limit that prevents higher income workers from getting their full proportional benefits. If there were no such feature, there would be a lot more "unemployment" than there is now.

Another way to look at it is to consider the net pay obtained for forty hours of work. If a man can get $93 for not working, and only $124 for working, then he is really working for only $31 per week. It isn't worth the effort. Why should he work for 78¢ per hour?

Not only must he work for peanuts, he may automatically lose his job skill classification and seniority, and all hope of getting his regular job back, if he takes a new job in a different occupation. Thus when a man is laid off, he usually waits for another job to open up in his own occupation and skill level, rather than risk permanent damage to his earning ability by such reclassifications. He doesn't really start looking for different kinds of work until his unemployment benefits are exhausted.

Thus we see that the present system of unemployment benefits produces a pattern of incentives which motivate a man to prolong his unemployment for various reasons. However we can change this system. Why not change it so that the benefits would motivate the unemployed to take some kind of a job, even a temporary job, as soon as possible? If we make it profitable for him to work, and if we protect him from any real risks to his future earning ability, we can in fact obtain the necessary change in his overall motivation pattern.

This change could be accomplished by a program which could be financed by the same wage tax used for the present system. Under the new system, if a man were laid off, he would go to the benefit office and make an application for his benefit. Here he would be given a long list of available "temporary jobs," most of which would probably pay at rates considerably below his normal wage rate.

However, the benefit would consist of a subsidy equal to half the difference between his temporary job rate and his regular job rate. Thus, if he normally makes $4.00 per hour, and the best temporary job he can get pays only $3.10 per hour, he would get an additional 45¢ from the government for every hour he works. In addition his name would be listed as available for work at his regular skill, and the government would legally guarantee all of his union rights, privileges, and seniority, as if he were still unemployed. All this would be included in the new system.

A further benefit would exist in that under the new system, his total dollar unemployment benefit eligibility would be maintained as it was in the old system. This means that his benefit might last several years instead of 26 weeks, since he is using it up at a much slower rate.

Taking the temporary job would not interfere with his getting back his old job if his company starts rehiring, and it would not interfere with obtaining another job at his regular skill if such should become available. For instance, suppose a job opened up at his regular skill but the other company pays only $3.80 per hour. He could take this job and still draw 10¢ per hour benefits until his eligibility runs out.

In fact the new system is designed to encourage him to find the very best temporary job he can get, since every pay increase means a higher total income until he is up to his former wage rate, at which time the subsidy automatically ceases. Even if he should get higher wages at his temporary job, the law would still protect his rights with regard to regaining his former job. However, if he refuses to accept the old job back again, if and when offered, he would then be considered to have terminated his special status, and his existing job would become his "regular" job, with regard to future benefits.

This system would virtually eliminate technological unemployment. The laid off worker would be immediately employed at the best job available, and he would have a higher income than provided by the present system of subsidizing unemployment. The worker would have greater security, since his benefits would last longer. In some cases, the temporary job might lead to greater opportunities and the worker would be much better off than in his former job. In cases where the old job never reappears, the worker would not waste futile years on welfare hoping for something that will never happen.

Thus our proposal is very simple. All *unemployment* benefits are eliminated. Instead, the worker would receive *employment* benefits. These benefits would be supplementary payments, for which he is eligible *after* he has accepted temporary employment. The amount of the benefit would be equal to half the difference between his regular pay rate, and the pay rate of the temporary job. In addition, his name would be carried on the list of those who are available for the next opening in his regular line of work, and the law would specify that all seniority rights, etc., would be guaranteed for the time he is eligible for the benefits under this program. The net effect of these provisions would be to cancel the hazard of losing his seniority, and would also reverse any economic incentive to remain unemployed. He would work because he would have to work to qualify for any benefits at all.

At first glance, it may seem hard to force a man to take a lower paying job, in order to receive his unemployment benefits. But actually it is not bad at all. He keeps his working habits and doesn't suffer the same frustrating feelings of futility and failure which he has being fully unemployed. His weekly spendable income will be considerably higher than they would be under the old system, and his coverage time will be greatly extended. If under the old system he had half pay for 26 weeks, then under the new system, if he could find a temporary job at even 50% of his regular pay, he could receive 75% of his regular pay as income plus benefits, and his eligibility would last for 52 weeks instead of 26 weeks. Not bad at all!

Help the Handicapped

In the thirties, unemployment was thought of as a blanket condition which could be eliminated or at least alleviated by the taxing and spending policies of the government. Today we are a little wiser and can recognize that some types of unemployment are little affected by these devices. If further progress is to be made, we must examine the several different types of unemployment which persist in the face of an overall labor shortage and increasing inflation.

The group that has the worst unemployment situation is the young people who are under 25. It is a surprise to most people that there is a higher percent of unemployment among white people under 25 than among black people over 25. At least two factors can be identified which cause this unemployment, and correction of either would provide an adequate remedy. One of these factors is the handicap of low productivity due to poor work habits, lack of skill, and improper education. The other factor is that the minimum wage rate is designed for heads of families rather than single adults.

In the past, the practice has been to shrug our shoulders and blame the lack of character, energy, intelligence, skill and responsibility of the individual, as if that took adequate care of the situation. If a man had only one arm, there would be compassion, and efforts would be made to find a job for him which he could handle. It is time we understand that handicaps can exist because of mental, emotional, racial, or educational reasons, and these also deserve compassionate treatment.

The present approach to this problem is to provide special (and costly) federal training programs, which are designed to improve skills sufficiently so that the man can find and hold a regular job. However these programs cannot serve more than a small fraction of today's young people and other handicapped people, as can be clearly seen from the persistence of this kind of unemployment, despite the billions spent on the various training programs. In time, of course, the individual problem generally solves itself and the man gets older, and perhaps a little wiser, and somehow finds a job. By this time he is likely to be over 25, so his ultimate success has no effect on the statistics describing the unemployment among young people under 25.

The other factor previously noted is the minimum wage laws. These laws were established on the basis that a man cannot adequately support a family if his wage is less than a certain minimum, presently believed to be about $3.10 per hour. Unfortunately, the law applies to all workers, not just the heads of families. Thus if a worker has a handicap that prevents him from producing value at least equal to the minimum wage, he cannot legally be employed unless the employer is willing to lose money on the deal.

However a single person does not require the full minimum wage to stay above the poverty level. Even at half the minimum, he is still getting twice as much on a per capita basis as a family of four with only one minimum wage paycheck coming in each payday. If we also recognize the fact that many single people are attached to other households and share the housing and utilities, etc., with others, it would appear that half of the minimum would yield a higher standard of living for a single person than does the full minimum wage for a head of a family.

Putting these ideas together, it is apparent that the minimum wage laws should be upgraded to account for the differing needs and for the differing abilities of people who are handicapped by insufficient productive capability, and who are not heads of families. To be specific, all single people who are under the age of 25 should have their legal minimum wage set at half the value which applies to ordinary workers. In addition there should be provision whereby any single worker, regardless of age, can apply for and obtain approval to work at half the regular minimum wage rate, if he can prove that he has a physical, mental, or emotional handicap which prevents him from achieving normal rates of productivity, or which causes him to be an unattractive risk for employment.

Many teenagers are employed in marginal jobs by small independent businessmen, shopkeepers, etc. When the minimum wage was raised from $1.25 in 1966 to $1.40 in 1967 and to $1.60 in 1968, there was a definite impact on the employment of teenagers. The National Federation of Independent Business representing more than 200,000 businesses, reported that about 40% of the employment reductions were caused by the increases in the minimum wage. The difference in wage cost between the two levels represents an increase in cost, (and a reduction in net profit) of $728 per year per worker.

What happens when such a marginal job is eliminated; who does the work? In many cases the work just doesn't get done. For instance many of the small businesses stopped delivery services, let the floors go unswept for longer periods, and cut back on their apprentice training programs.

The opposite effect would occur if the youth exemption were to be put into effect. Jobs would again exist for delivery boys, part-time window washers, floor sweepers, and assistant clerks. More services would be supplied to increase our standard of living, and the teenagers would have ways of earning money and keeping out of trouble. Best of all they would be completing an important part of their education which is how to get along with the boss, how to earn a living, and how to be a responsible member of the community.

Employing Overtime

Business activity varies. This variation is inevitable, whether we consider any individual business or the economy as a whole. As long as we permit the inevitable variations in business activity to impose variations in unemployment, we cannot solve the unemployment problem. What we need is a system where unemployment is not affected by variations in business activity.

However the variations in business activity do require a variation in the number of manhours worked each week. There are two ways to meet this variable demand. One way is to vary the number of people employed. The other way is to vary the number of hours worked by each employee. If we wish to minimize unemployment, we must find a way to motivate employers to meet the demand for labor by varying the number of hours worked by individual employees rather than varying the number of employees by layoffs and rehirings.

Since 1936, we have had the Wages and Hours Law which requires employers to pay extra whenever employees work more than the standard forty hour work week. The effect of this law is to change the behavior of employers, depending on whether the actual work week of their employees is above or below the forty hour standard. When the actual work week is below the standard, the employer can reduce his overhead costs by reducing the number of people on the payroll. Thus his motivation is to lay some off and let the rest work the full forty hours. But when the actual work week is above the standard, he can save money by reducing the overtime. Under this condition the motivation is to keep his work force intact and hire more workers if he can find them.

The common perception is that when business activity increases, workers are hired, and when it decreases, workers are laid off. But in the individual case, the actual policy of the employer is determined by whether or not his overall profits are increased by hiring or by laying people off, and this is directly affected by whether or not his people are working overtime. If they are on overtime, he will be reluctant to lay anyone off, regardless of whether business is going up or down. It is only when his people are working less than the standard week that he can save money by laying people off.

Therefore if we wish to prevent layoffs, an effective way to do so would be to reduce the standard enough so that the average work week always exceeds the standard work week, producing a condition where most employers are paying overtime, even during periods of business recession.

The lowest level of unemployment that has been attained in this country was the 1.2% experienced during the middle of World War II. This could represent a goal for minimized unemployment. If we subtract this from the post war high of 8.5%, we can see that our objective is to soak up at least 7.3% unemployment.

Other things being equal, a 7.3% increase in employment can be accommodated by a reduction of about 2.7 hours in the average work week. Therefore if the standard work week were changed to 37.3 hours, there would be an overtime incentive to hire more workers which would persist until this 7.3% excess unemployment was eliminated. Setting the standard a little lower, say at 36 hours per week, would provide a little more incentive. Setting the standard at 32 hours per week would impose a very strong incentive, and would rapidly reduce the unemployment to residual levels which have only existed during wartime emergencies.

In the condition of minimized unemployment, there would be an intense labor shortage and prevalent overtime, exactly the employment conditions that existed in 1944. Some workers would be working eight hours or more overtime, others somewhat less, and a few would be working straight time. The only difference between these conditions and those of 1944 would be that the actual number of hours worked each week would be less than in 1944. In other words, we would have reproduced all of the conditions that produce and accompany minimized unemployment except at a lower number of hours each week.

If this analysis is valid, then it ought to be reflected in our historical records. After all, the work week has varied above and below the 40 hour standard many times. Therefore we should be able to show that when the actual work week went above the 40 hour standard, there was a drop in unemployment as employers were forced to pay overtime. Also we should find that when the work week dropped below the standard, unemployment should jump up, reflecting the greater tendency for employers to lay people off.

Figure 1 shows the record back to the 1940's. Since the end of the Great Depression, the actual work week has dropped below the 40 hour standard six times, and each time the unemployment rate jumped to over 5.5%. In between, when the work week rose above the standard, unemployment went down. The record is consistent with our prediction. The existence of overtime is a powerful motivation which minimizes unemployment.

Although we have focused on the behavior of employers, unemployment is also affected by that of employees. People who quit increase unemployment as well as people who are laid off. What would be the effect of prevalent overtime on the behavior of employees?

One effect would result from the fact that some employers would be paying more overtime than others, simply because their business demand for labor is higher. Although the employees that would be working only a straight time 32 hour week might be thankful that they were not unemployed, some, at least, would be dissatisfied with the lower take home pay, especially when they compare their situation with that of other workers. Fortunately, there would be no problem in finding a job with more overtime, since the employer with the high overtime costs would be most anxious to hire some new employees.

Thus we could expect such workers to find jobs in other businesses, or even in other geographical areas where overtime is more prevalent. This would be healthy since it would increase the general mobility of the labor force to accommodate geographical as well as temporal variations in business activity. The overall effect would be to even out the amount of overtime, and thus more equally share both the wealth and the leisure that is the result of a successful capitalistic society.

The benefits of this proposal are obvious, but what about the disadvantages? Are there some side effects that would cancel out the benefits? Would it be accepted by those who make our laws and run our economy?

The major disadvantage of this proposal to minimize unemployment is that it would in fact minimize the unemployment!

Do union leaders really want to get rid of the unemployment problem? What if that reduces the need for their services? Do politicians really want to eliminate the fear of unemployment? How would they justify the useless expenditure of government funds? Do businessmen really want to eliminate the fear of unemployment? How would they intimidate their employees? The very fact that unemployment is minimized and the fear of unemployment eliminated would be considered highly disadvantageous to many of the important people who make our laws and run our economy.

In addition to these, switching over to an overtime economy will produce many other changes which will benefit some and disadvantage others.

Business costs will be increased by the additional overhead as more people go on the payroll. Costs will also increase because of the extra overtime. However costs for the taxes that fund the unemployment insurance program will go down. Also demand for goods will go up, partly because the new employees will have more money to spend, and partly because everyone will have more leisure time, which means more sports equipment, more tourist business, etc. The overall result should be a higher material standard of living as well as a better quality of life.

In summary, many of the changes will be most beneficial to the general public, but some will be disadvantageous to powerful interests. Unfortunately, the politicians would be affected worst of all, since they could no longer gather easy votes by showing their "concern" for the problem, and they could no longer justify patronage projects by claiming that they are needed to "fight unemployment." Since it is the politicians who must change the law to make all this possible, we can be sure that it will never happen unless the people insist!

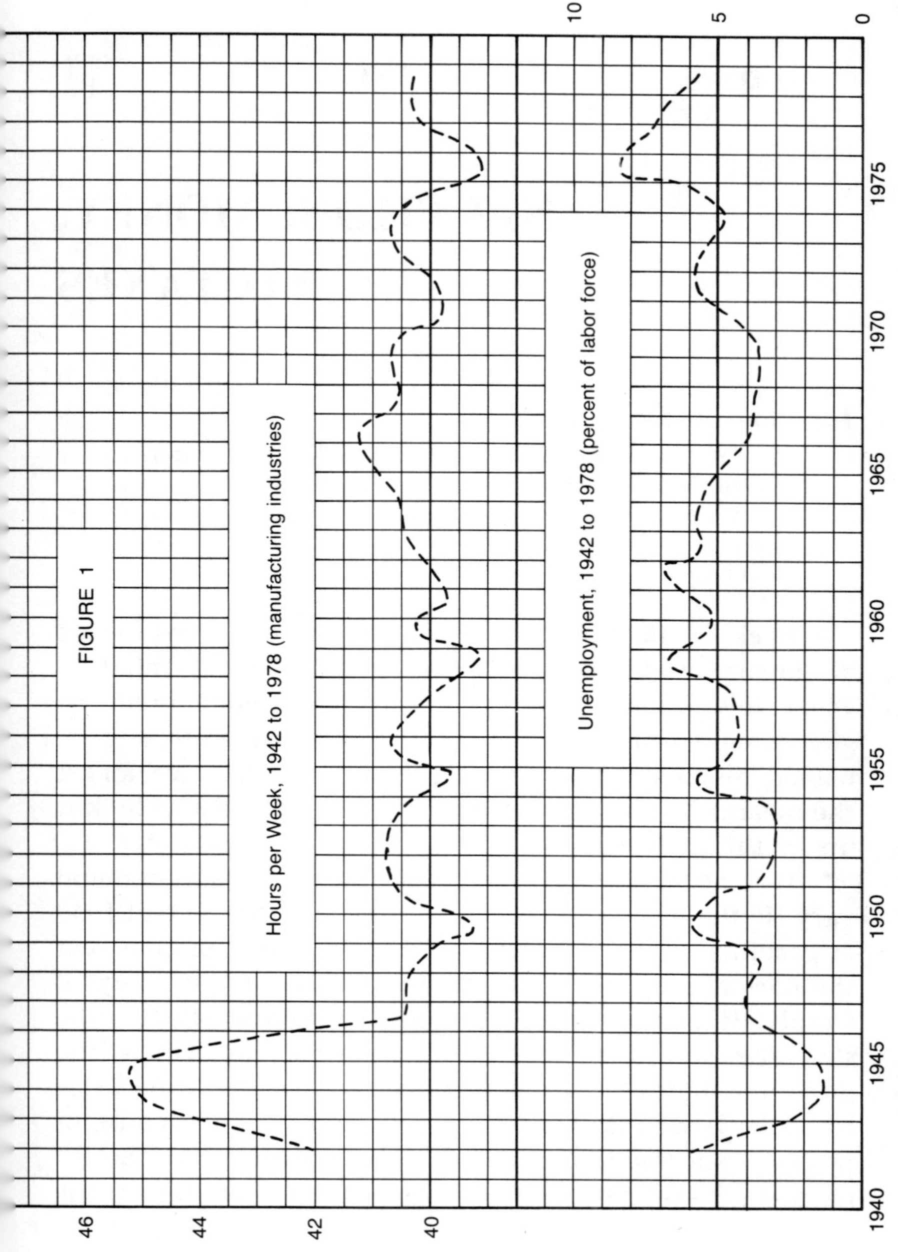
FIGURE 1
Hours per Week, 1942 to 1978 (manufacturing industries)
Unemployment, 1942 to 1978 (percent of labor force)
46
44
42
40
10
5
0
1940
1945
1950
1955
1960
1965
1970
1975

II

INFLATION, MONEY, AND TAXES

Taxation by Deception

> "Inflate: To expand or increase abnormally, or improperly, to extend imprudently, as to inflate the volume of money and credit so that a general rise in price level occurs . . ." (Webster's New International Dictionary, second edition)

Back in 1948 when the second edition of Webster's dictionary was published, people knew what inflation was. Now no one seems to know! TV commentators, government economists, news analysts, all profess to be baffled by this mysterious affliction. How can we forget the meaning of a word when all we have to do is to look it up in the dictionary?

It is normal for prices to vary as supply and demand vary. If the price rises because there is a shortage of food or gasoline, that is *not* inflation. Such a rise in price is just the normal response of the free market to any shortage of supply. If prices did not respond to such shortages, the shortage would persist, as always occurs when the government tries to prevent price rises by imposing price controls. If we insist on confusing the normal response of prices to shortages of particular commodities with the abnormal general rise in prices caused by the inflation of the supply of money and credit, we will never be able to solve the problem of inflation. But if we can understand that inflation simply means the increase in the supply of money and credit, then the solution to the problem becomes very obvious. The way to stop inflation is to stop the increase in the supply of money and credit. It is as simple as that!

Of course every economist working for the government knows this to be true, he could not have passed his first course in economics without this basic concept. So why don't they tell the people the simple truth? Why the massive cover up? Why must they try to place the blame on business, on labor, on the housewife, on "all of us"?

The answer of course is obvious. The economists work for the politicians and the politicians do not want to eliminate inflation. They want to continue to use inflation as a convenient way to enrich themselves and their friends and to maintain and increase their power. Inflation is the silent tax, but it cannot be effective unless the people are deceived. Inflation is taxation by deception.

But it is not an equal tax. Some pay heavily, others pay less, some make money on the system. For instance every home owner who borrows money at low interest rates and pays it back with inflated currency is making money from the system. If the inflation rate is 10% and his mortgage rate is 8%, he is being paid 2% to use the money. When you consider that he can also deduct the interest payments from his taxable income, it is clear that he is making a lot of money from the inflation.

Speculators and middlemen also make money from inflation. Their code word is OPM, meaning other people's money. As long as the inflation rate is equal or greater than the interest rate, they can borrow money and buy almost anything and make a profit.

If all of these people benefit from inflation, who is hurt? The people who are hurt the most are the disadvantaged, the old, the poor, and the trusting. Inflation defrauds those who are trying to live on their savings, social security, pensions, or insurance.

In addition to these, inflation robs every person who invests in stocks, bonds, or mortgages. The combination of inflation and the income tax has made it impossible to find a reasonably safe investment that does not lose money. Good investments lose less, bad investments lose more, but all reasonably safe investments lose money after accounting for taxes and inflation.

But what about the bankers? Bankers are in business to loan out money. Doesn't inflation hurt them too?

There is one important difference. Bankers do not loan out their own money, they loan other people's money. It is those other people who suffer the losses from inflation. The banker makes money, and since inflation increases the demand for loans, bankers make more from inflation, a lot more.

What the bankers especially like is when the government creates more "reserves" by running a budget deficit. These deficits create more government bonds which, by fiscal magic, are legally equivalent to additional reserves of gold. Thus for every dollar borrowed by the government, the banks get to loan out three or four additional dollars. The money for these loans doesn't even exist until the loan is made. It is created out of thin air and it disappears when the loan is paid back. But the interest "earned" by the bank is real enough.

Thus our inflation is nothing more than a gigantic scheme for legal counterfeiting, with the bankers printing the money, with the politicians getting "free" dollars to give to their friends and supporters, and with the bankers getting several times as many dollars to loan out at high rates of interest. Of all the people who profit from inflation it is the politicians and their banker friends who profit the most.

Once we understand that it is the politicians and the bankers who profit the most from inflation it shouldn't be surprising to find that it is also the politicians and bankers who actually do the inflating. Some of the details of this unholy arrangement are quite interesting.

The Constitution (Art. I, Sect. 8) gives Congress the power to coin money and regulate the value thereof. But Congress doesn't do this anymore. In 1913, Congress set up the Federal Reserve System and turned over the power to regulate the value of our money to the bankers. This gave the bankers the legal monopoly to create money, to manipulate the quantity of money, to manipulate interest rates and reserve requirements, and to inflate or deflate at their own discretion. They operate in secret with no audit or outside accounting, and with no real oversight by Congress.

The Federal Reserve Board meets in secret and decides future monetary policies that have the effect of driving the stock and bond markets up or down as they may decide. This gives them and their friends advance knowledge which may or may not be used for private gain. All inflations we have experienced since 1913 have been the result of deliberate decisions by these men, and all recessions and depressions, including the big one of 1929 have been triggered by actions taken by the FRB to tighten credit. As long as the general public is ignorant of the awesome powers that Congress has given to the bankers, there is little chance of any major change. The FRB will continue to manipulate our money and our markets in accordance with their own judgment and interest.

Under the present law, Congress cannot really control inflation if the FRB insists on inflating. Under present law, the power is with the FRB. If by some miracle, Congress does decide to reduce inflation, the only way that it can do so would be to modify the powers that it has delegated to the FRB. One way would be to pass a law that would require the FRB to hold the supply of money and credit constant within narrow specified limits, with stiff penalties placed on the members of the FRB if they do not comply with the law. Theoretically they could do that at any time. Practically it is virtually impossible for Congress to go against the interests of the bankers.

It costs a lot of money to run for Congress. Those who are elected are the ones who can attract a lot of money for their campaign. Along with the doctors, the bankers give the most money to the incumbent congressmen of both parties. This money is very welcome, but it also carries a silent threat. Any congressman who goes against the interests of the bankers can find that the money needed to finance his campaign is going to his opponent. When the new congressman takes office, he is unlikely to oppose the interests of his generous friends, the bankers.

Of course if all of the congressmen acted together, they could probably take the needed action without too much risk for any single member. But no one wants to be first, and so the power of the banking lobby continues unchallenged.

But most congressmen do not really want to eliminate inflation. Inflation provides them with free money to give to their people. With inflation, Congress doesn't have to raise taxes, taxes are automatically raised as inflation pushes people into higher income brackets. Thus they not only pay more, they have to pay a higher percentage of their income.

In addition to the larger revenue from the income tax, Congress can also spend still more money by going into debt. If they had to borrow all that money from a fixed supply of existing dollars, it might be quite difficult and perhaps at times impossible. But with the present cozy relationship with the Federal Reserve, there is no problem. If the public will not buy the government bonds, the FRB will.

So we see that Congress and the bankers are really one team, cooperating together in an incredibly complicated and ingenious ripoff of the public. Congress votes the deficits, the Federal Reserve prints the money, and our news commentators blame the greedy housewife for buying too much food and clothing. This is the basic cause of our inflation, and it will continue until the public wakes up and does something about it.

Credit Control

As noted previously, inflation is simply the increase in the supply of money and credit. Therefore any action that will reduce the formation of either additional money or credit will reduce inflation. Even though the power to increase or reduce the money supply has been taken over by the bankers, there are still some useful things that could be done, if we want to fight inflation, by simply reducing the rate of increase of credit. This applies to both the public and the private sectors.

In the public sector, most people are familiar with the Proposition 13 type of proposals to force governments to limit their taxes and to balance their budgets. This movement has had success with State governments, and is now working to force some needed reforms on the national level. The main thrust is to try to force Congress to balance the Federal Budget each year, by amending the Constitution if necessary.

Unfortunately, even if they are successful, they will find that just balancing the budget does not mean elimination of deficit spending. After all a budget is just an estimate of receipts and an authorization of expenditures. Year by year Congress exceeds its own budget, whether innocently or intentionally. So even if there were a requirement to balance the budget, Congress could easily get around it by estimating receipts high and expenditures low.

One way to solve that problem would be to require that actual expenditures shall not exceed the previous year's receipts. We should use the previous year's receipts because these are a matter of record and can be verified and attested. If we say current year receipts, then we have no way to know whether the requirement is being met or not, until after it is all over. So the proponents of mandatory balanced budgets should write this essential requirement into their proposals so that expenditures will not be allowed to exceed the receipts for the previous fiscal year.

In the private sector, inflation could be reduced significantly if Congress would pass laws to limit consumer credit. One way is to require a minimum down payment that is larger than customary. In effect, this is a requirement that less credit be extended for each purchase. Another way is to require repayment in fewer years. This reduces the time for each loan, thus reducing the overall volume of credit. Measures such as these were employed quite successfully to control rapid inflation during the Korean War.

Another opportunity for limiting consumer credit would be to review all Federal loan guarantee programs, many of which provide loans at interest rates below commercial rates and below current inflation rates. Such loans encourage borrowing, whether or not the money is needed, since the borrower can actually make money by depositing the money in higher yield certificates of deposit and pocket the difference in the interest rates. To avoid such abuse, all Federal loans should be at interest rates at least as high as the current rate of inflation.

With the rise of the credit card, there has been an explosion of consumer credit which directly contributes to the overall inflation. Thus a convenient way to reduce inflation would be to reduce the use of credit cards. This could be done either by increasing the rate of interest charged or by reducing the rate charged. If the rate were set high enough, people could not afford to use them. If the rate were set too low, the banks could not afford to provide the service. It would appear that the best approach would be to reduce the rate of interest that can be charged on credit cards from the present 18% down to about 12%. This would probably reduce the use of credit cards significantly without eliminating them entirely. Those who really need the service could still get it by paying directly for the use of the card when it is issued.

Foundations of Evasion

Most people think of money in terms of things that they would like to buy, if they only had a little more of it. However, as soon as one gets a little more prosperous, he finds that he has been buying this and that, and he really has more stuff than he can keep track of. One answer is to buy a larger house with bigger closets. Then you need a maid to help the wife with the cleaning, and pretty soon you need a housekeeper to keep track of the maid, etc. If and when you get tired of buying little stuff, you can always buy big stuff, perhaps an airplane or a boat. And so it goes.

However if you are a busy rich man you will find, sooner or later, that you don't really enjoy all these toys as much as you had expected, and you get a little bored. Playing with things is childish, the real fun is in playing with people.

The Foundation is an ideal way to pretend that you do not have any money when the tax collector comes around, and at the same time have the full use of it for your new hobby of influencing other peoples' lives. Since you don't need the money to buy things with anymore, the friendly government lets you keep control of it, pay no taxes at all, pile up the tax-free earnings, and have complete control of what it is used for except, of course, you mustn't use it to buy any more toys for yourself.

In other words, the main value of money to those who are not rich, lies in its power to obtain goods for personal consumption. The main value of money for those who are quite rich, lies in the power that it gives them over other people.

When we look at it this way, we see that the "non profit" family foundations are simply a method for evading taxes, while retaining all of the important advantages of being rich. As soon as this becomes clear to a majority of voters, they will demand that the foundations be taxed just like any other holding corporation. When this occurs, the tax levied on ordinary people can be reduced, and it will cost a little more for rich people to indulge their hobby of molding our opinions and controlling our future.

What About Tariffs?

The thing about tariffs is that although all of us are just as much consumers as producers, we are much better organized as producers than as consumers. Since tariffs benefit producers, and hurt consumers, the pro-tariff propaganda put out by ourselves, organized as producers, drowns out our pitiful cry as consumers. However, the fact remains that tariffs are generally bad for the country as a whole in that the harm to consumers greatly exceeds the benefits to the producers.

If we assume a linear price-demand elasticity, it is obvious that fewer goods will be sold at higher prices with the tariff in effect than at the lower prices when the tariff is abolished. Thus even if the producers' gain for each item equaled the consumers' loss, the fact that more would be consumed at the lower price means that the overall good for the greatest number would be increased by abolishing the tariff.

Not only do tariffs reduce consumption, they also hold down production. If imports are consumed, foreign companies earn dollars. Assuming they do not want to keep these dollars forever, the only thing they can do with them is to come back to this country and buy other goods and services. If they keep the dollars and refuse to buy our products, we get their goods free of charge. It is just as intelligent for a foreign country to sell us their stuff for dollars, and keep the dollars, as it would be for an auto dealer to sell you a new car and then refuse to deposit your check into his bank account!

Now it is true that foreign countries will often erect tariff barriers against us. Some of these barriers are due to their own lack of understanding: we have no monopoly on stupidity. Some of them are due to their internal power struggles, with one group of producers trying to defraud the others. Some of them are honest attempts to conserve their dollars for purposes that the leaders, rightly or wrongly, consider vital for their country. Ascribing malicious motives to other peoples' tariffs is not very intelligent nor does it have any useful consequences. Tariffs cannot be essentially malicious, only stupid. It is like a small child banging his head against the wall to make his mother feel bad.

Since tariffs hurt the country that imposes them more than the countries against whom they are raised, the whole concept of reciprocity has as much sense as for one child to promise another that he will stop banging his head against the wall if the other child will stop, too. Multilateral tariff agreements are even more ridiculous. We will all stop banging our heads together!

The only sensible approach is to just eliminate your own tariffs, and enjoy the increased standard of living. Sure, you would like the other countries to reduce their tariffs too; increased trade benefits everybody. But this is more likely to occur by demonstrating the reality of the benefits with our own sensible example than by trying to bully the other countries into doing something that really is for their own good anyway. As long as we try to argue them into doing it, they will continue to believe that maybe tariff reduction really isn't in their own best interests.

All of this supposes that the foreign country does, in fact, have no malicious intent. Countries with an announced plan of world conquest obviously do not qualify as being free of malicious intent. In a conflict situation, trading with the enemy is wrong, even if it is profitable, since you are also profiting the enemy and putting yourself at his mercy with regard to his increased ability to disrupt your economy when he so chooses.

All of the détente policies with the Russian Communists may soon be seen as the essential factor in their victory. We have opened our country to them as did Hezekiah, King of Judah, to the "friendly" emissaries from Babylon. That demonstration of trust and détente led to the slaughter and captivity of his entire nation by the Babylonians, as you can read for yourself in II Kings 20:12-18.

Thus, the proper strategy for tariffs is quite simple. Eliminate them unilaterally as far as friendly nations are concerned, but increase them to stop as much trade as possible with those who intend to conquer us. If the Russians are to bury us, let's make it as difficult as possible!

Import controls are often substituted for tariffs. These same principles hold true as long as the volume of imports do not cause massive variations in the domestic market. If such variations are expected, then an automatic stabilizing control system, as discussed in the chapter on regulating commerce, would be in order.

The Automated Gold Standard

The best currency for international trade is one which is fully convertible into gold at a fixed rate of exchange. With such a currency, buyers and sellers can agree on terms knowing that when the payment is made, the money will be worth exactly the same as it was when the contract was signed.

For many years the British Pound Sterling met this requirement and thus became the preferred currency for international transactions. When the Pound was devalued, the gold convertible U.S. Dollar became the currency of choice. But the constant printing of paper dollar bills, far in excess of the gold reserve, led to the complete devaluation of the dollar in 1972. Now the world has no gold convertible currency for international trade, and the value of the various paper currencies varies constantly and unpredictably.

Some have suggested that the U.S. should go back on the gold standard by setting a new official price for gold and promising to maintain that price indefinitely by suitably internal taxation and deflationary policies. Certainly such promises could be made. But who would believe us? In the past we made a similar promise to redeem dollar bills with gold at $20.67 per oz. Then in 1934 we changed it to $35 per oz. defrauding the owners of 41% of their holdings. Then in 1972, we refused to redeem dollars for gold at any price.

History shows that no government can permanently fix the price of anything, and this includes the price of gold. To be successful, a price fixer must have complete control of either the supply or the demand. Theoretically, it would seem that a national government would have this required degree of control over the quantity of paper currency which it issues. Actually this control is an illusion, since in practice the adverse effects of contracting the money supply will endanger the existence of the government itself. This is the basic reason why governments have abandoned the fixed price gold standard money system. But if the fixed price gold standard is not practical, what is?

The most important requirement for an acceptable international currency is predictability of value. If the value can be predicted, sellers can know the exact value that will be received for the goods being furnished, even though payment may be made months after the signing of the contract.

In order for a currency to have a predictable value, it must be immune to manipulations and devaluations. This means that its value must not depend on future decisions to be made by anyone, especially not by bankers and politicians. Some other desirable qualities would be universal availability and acceptability, but these would naturally follow if the currency did indeed have a reliable predictability of value.

It would also be desirable for the currency to have constancy of value. This would allow its use as a means for storing value indefinitely. But this quality, however desirable, is not really essential. For the purposes of facilitating trade, it is enough to have a reliable predictability of value during the life of a contract. Actual constancy of value is not required.

The dollar could be adapted to meet these requirements if legislation were enacted that would make the dollar convertible to gold on a sliding price scale. At the start, the official exchange price would be set at the then current free market price. The law would specify a predetermined sliding scale for the dollar price of gold which would depend on the inventory of gold in the U.S. Treasury. The sliding scale would be set such that whenever the inventory of gold goes down 1%, the price goes up 2%. Similarly, when the inventory of gold rises 1%, the price goes down 2%. The law would also specify that the price charged for gold sold by the Treasury will be 2% above the price paid for gold bought, for any given level of gold inventory. All prices would be based on the inventory that exists after the day's trading is completed.

By setting the selling price a fixed percentage above the purchase price, every time there is a price reversal the Treasury would make a profit on all the gold that was sold and repurchased. This profit by the Treasury means a net overall loss for speculators, and this would tend to discourage short term fluctuations in the dollar-gold exchange price level. However long term trends would be automatically accommodated and the official price of gold would faithfully reflect any persisting inflation or deflation of the dollar.

The reason for making the price vary twice as fast, and in the opposite direction, as the inventory change is to provide for an automatic stabilization effect. If demand for our gold becomes very high, the price will go up enough to discourage additional purchases before too much gold is lost from our inventory. Similarly if large supplies are offered, the reduced price will discourage additional selling. The desired result is a relatively constant inventory of gold, and a relatively constant or slowly varying price. We want to damp out all the short term variations with long term changes occurring slowly and predictably.

After a period of operation, the record of the trends in the official price of gold would be available for analysis by the public. Statistical analysis of the behavior of the dollar-gold price curve would yield informed predictions of future behavior as well as the expected accuracy of such predictions. Using such analysis as a basis, traders could reduce to a minimum the uncertainty expected in the real value of future dollar receipts, and the result would be a significant reduction in the risks associated with international trade and investment.

In addition to this benefit, there would also be the benefit of having a convenient and impartial measurement of domestic inflation. If a future administration does really try to control inflation, its success would be readily demonstrated by a flattening out of the dollar-gold exchange curve. On the other hand, irresponsible administrations would have their failures held up for all to see.

In summary, there is a third choice besides the fixed price gold standard and the free floating paper money systems. By linking the dollar to gold on a sliding scale, we can obtain the essential predictability of value that is associated with the fixed price gold standard, and also obtain the capability for automatic accommodation to long term changes in the free market price of gold. In a sense, we obtain the best advantages of each system while avoiding the worst disadvantages of both.

III

STREET CRIME

Cause or Cure?

In medieval times the recommended cure for disease was to bleed the patient. Those who followed the expert medical advice of that time died faster than those who depended on their own common sense. Today we know that the medical doctors were dead wrong. But how could you tell if you were a sick person in 1342 A.D.?

The medieval doctors had no monopoly on error, and error is not at all limited to the medical profession. Any "expert" can be wrong! The problem today is the same as it was then. How do we know when to believe the experts-in-the-field, and how do we know when to stop believing them? Perhaps we can formulate a general rule to guide us in this difficult decision.

The rule is quite simple. If the experts are right, we can expect to find problems being solved, predictions being confirmed, and conditions improving. However if problems are not being solved and predictions are failing, and conditions continue to deteriorate, then one has a right to suspect that the experts may in fact be wrong. And when the situation gets worse in proportion to the effort made to correct the problem, this is a signal that the methods being employed are probably part of the problem. In the medical profession there is even a particular word for this type of situation, "iatrogenic," meaning diseases caused by the doctor.

In past years, with primitive technology, the law enforcement system was somehow able to keep the streets safe enough so that the cities attracted people rather than frightened them away. People could walk the streets without undue fear. Modern penal theory scorns the simplistic methods used in the past, but for the ordinary citizen on the street, it was a lot safer then than it is now.

Today we have street crime out of control. Muggings, beatings, rape, robbery, and casual murder are common occurrences. People are afraid to go out at night, in fact they are not really safe on the streets during the day. People who can leave the city do so, often with great financial hardship and inconvenience. Those who cannot leave become prisoners in their own homes. This situation is intolerable, and it is time that we do something about it. We must get rid of street crime.

Many people look to the police for this needed improvement. Police effectiveness can be improved, and some specific proposals for such improvement are submitted in this chapter. But we should recognize that the police are already doing a pretty fair job, and further improvements cannot really solve the overall problem of street crime. It is the courts which fail to administer justice, and the correctional system, which fails to either deter or rehabilitate, that require the major reform.

The courts have permitted delay tactics, technicalities, and convenience for the lawyers to make a mockery of their attempts to administer justice. Many courts no longer even pretend to administer equal justice. Equal justice is an obsolete concept according to modern theory. Instead, the court will treat the criminal offender as an unfortunate victim of a cruel society, and address itself to what is best for the criminal rather than how to protect society.

From a systems point of view, the trouble is that

there is no feedback, that is, the courts seem unable to correct their own errors. There is no one in charge, there are no rewards for competent performance and no punishment for poor performance. Thus the courts operate as a law unto themselves, and they have no effective means for self discipline.

The correctional system has bogged down in a quagmire of conflicting purposes and unrealistic goals. Originally the purpose was punishment as vengence for wrong doing. Later it was recognized that the important thing is to deter, to make the convict afraid to repeat his crime, and to make others fear the consequences if they commit similar offences. Still later ideas were entertained as to the need for the isolation of dangerous men from open society as a direct means for preventing future offences. Last and presently most fashionable are the ideas regarding the reformation and rehabilitation of the offender so that he will be able to "go straight."

All of these correctional objectives have some validity, but unfortunately, the requirements for these different purposes tend to conflict with and nullify each other. The overall result is impotence and confusion, and today it is generally recognized that the correctional institutions do more harm than good. The correctional system openly admits this failure, and the latest correctional strategy is to minimize the time that a convict spends in the institution. The objective is to release him on parole as soon as possible. This may or may not aid in rehabilitation of the convict, but one thing is certain, it does keep the criminal on the street where he can repeat his offences at his own choosing.

Over and over we hear the constant theme of the correctional establishment which is that they could do a much better job if only the public would arise from its apathy and give them more money. We hear this statement at the very time that the polls show that the most intense concern of the public is for protection against street crime. Apathy is definitely not the problem. The real problem is that the public is paying for protection and not getting it because the correctional agencies prefer to continue their futile efforts to forcibly "rehabilitate" criminal offenders rather than to put priority on the protection of the public.

Human nature is very hard to change. When the methods of law enforcement are well adapted to human nature, it is not particularly difficult to achieve an acceptable level of public security without excessive taxation. But when we get too smart for ourselves and decide to go against human nature, we find that the harder we try, the more trouble we get ourselves into. This is one reason why we are losing ground in our war against street crime.

The unique responsibility of government is to protect people from fraud, violence, and coercion by other people. Its duty is to establish law, order, and equal justice. In order to do this important task it is given awesome powers, powers that include the legitimate use of violence, confiscation of property, imprisonment, punishment, and even the right to take life itself. It is important that these powers be restricted narrowly to the task for which they are granted. Use of such powers to dominate peoples individuality, to forcibly remold their character, or to wash their brains to a slavish conformity, is totally inappropriate in a free society.

The specific proposals submitted in this chapter are designed to be practical. The intent is to work with rather than against human nature. The idea is to stop beating away at unrewarding side goals and concentrate on the main goal of achieving an acceptable level of public safety. Let's get rid of street crime!

Improving the Police Image

To operate effectively, the police need the trust and cooperation of at least some of the people with whom they interface. Whether or not they get this cooperation depends mainly on the image, the picture that comes to mind when one thinks of the police. If the police are thought of as brutal oppressors, or as unpredictable strangers, the people will remain passive or even hostile. What is necessary is that the police be accepted as friendly protectors of the people of the neighborhood.

Despite the difficulties and limitations associated with the cop-on-the-beat system, there are essential advantages that cannot be reproduced by any other substitute no matter how sophisticated. The policeman walking on the beat gets to know the local people and they get to know him. If he has any qualifications at all, some of the local people will consider him as an ally rather than as an enemy, and they will provide the moral support which is so necessary for the effective protection of the neighborhood.

Once the policeman gets to know the people, he will find that he gets information. If he is competent, he will make sure that those who help him with such information are not harassed by legalities and unwanted summons, or put on public view for revenge by the criminals who are caught as a result of such information. When the people understand that cooperation with a particular policeman does not lead to adverse involvement, there will be a strong motivation for the people in the neighborhood to help the patrolman as much as they can. After all, it is their lives and property that he is trying to protect. The powerful motives of self preservation are thus aligned with, rather than against the law enforcement effort.

If the foot patrol is so valuable, why have most of the police forces switched over to patrol cars? There is no doubt that the patrol cars provide many important advantages, measurable advantages. They give fast mobility, instant two way communication, and they provide considerable personal protection from bodily assault as long as the policeman stays in the squad car. But the obvious advantages have matching disadvantages which are not so obvious and cannot be easily measured.

Fast mobility may mean that the law does not stay long enough in any one place to detect a crime, even when it is just taking place. Increased communication with headquarters also means decreased communications with the people in the neighborhood. And when the police stay inside their patrol cars, the people come to believe that they are afraid to walk the street. This inevitably turns respect into contempt. If the police are afraid to walk the street, how can we expect ordinary citizens not to be in constant fear? If the police cannot safely walk the streets, who can?

But there are ways to obtain most of the advantages of the patrol cars and make them available for the use of the foot patrol. We have very efficient light weight two way radios today. These should be a standard part of every patrolman's equipment. Where such units are not powerful enough to reach headquarters, automatic relay stations could be set up in strategic locations, or even carried by regionally based squad cars.

It is essential that the police be racially acceptable in a neighborhood, especially where there are racial tensions and antagonisms. Integration and color blindness may be useful ideals but when the safety of a patrol officer is concerned, there is no sense in rubbing people the wrong way. The police officer must be fully accepted by the people that he is trying to protect.

Those who patrol the most dangerous neighborhoods, should go in pairs and should check in at frequent intervals with their two way radios. They should also be supplied with a light weight body armor under their uniforms as additional protection against sniper fire from fanatics and terrorists. If all of these provisions are made, the foot patrol will have sufficient personal security that it can establish the physical presence of the law, even in the most dangerous crime ridden areas.

The foot patrol should be considered as the most important part of the police force. Those who are assigned to the foot patrol should be the very best, physically, mentally, and emotionally. They should have expert capability in judo and karate, so that they do not have to use their weapons unnecessarily. They should be tested to make sure that their personality, knowledge and attitudes are such as to help them win community acceptance. Those who qualify for service in the foot patrol should be given the extra pay and respect which they deserve. This way, the foot patrol will have the glamour and prestige which are necessary to attract the competent people needed for this most important service.

The main reason why the foot patrol has been abandoned is that it is easier to measure the effectiveness of the squad car than the foot patrol. The statistics thus favor the squad car. Recently, the Federal Government financed a study program, putting the foot patrol back into service in some dangerous neighborhoods in St. Louis during 1972 to 1975. The project was finally abandoned because of cost and "inconclusive statistical findings." The report indicates that although the patrol probably caused an overall reduction in crime, the immediate presence of the police caused more arrests as criminals were actually caught in the act. Therefore the statisticians could not point to a reduced arrest rate and their conclusion was that the results were "inconclusive." But they were not inconclusive to the people of the neighborhoods that were protected. An overwhelming 83% of the citizens of these neighborhoods were in favor of continuing the program even if it meant an increase in their own taxes as the Federal support was phased out.

Back in the depths of the Great Depression, we were somehow able to afford the costs of providing effective police protection including the foot patrol. The result was a low crime rate and safe streets for everyone. Now, after forty years of prosperity and a rising standard of living, we cannot afford this basic police protection!

Another way in which the image of the police could be improved would be for one of the daily newspapers to donate one full page each day for the exclusive use of the police department. It would be up to the police to fill up this space with information of interest and value to the community. An infinite variety of information can be visualized, including:

1. Review of criminal cases at the time the punishment begins, emphasizing the causal effect between the crime and the punishment.
2. Publicizing services rendered and people protected.
3. How are we doing statistics, enlisting interest and support in a competition with other cities in the fight to reduce criminal incidents and to minimize unpunished crimes.
4. Showing pictures of local criminals wanted for questioning on an immediate day to day basis.
5. Recruiting advertisements.
6. Charts showing disposition of arrests, legal delays, and obstructions which prevent prompt justice.
7. "Letters to the Cops" column, where citizens can voice complaints and get direct and public answers from the Chief of Police.
8. Pointing up specific needs, such as equipment, men, cooperation, voluntary traffic diversion, etc.
9. Educational material on proper safeguarding of property, restrictions and regulations on personal arms, fraudulent business practices, confidence games being practiced, tax liabilities, auto inspection and licensing information, etc.
10. Awards of prizes, certificates, or medals for outstanding service or heroic performance, including both citizens and police officers.

Giving a free page to the police bypasses the inevitable filtration of the news by the reporter and the copy editor. Their interest is in obtaining maximum transient interest from a "story." This conflicts with the objective of presenting information so as to enlist the active support of the citizens against crime. The most notorious example of this conflict is the sob story, where interest is created and sympathy generated for the criminal, and the victim's problems are totally ignored. If the police themselves have to write the story, the public may have more sympathy for the victim and less for the criminal.

The image would also be improved if the police were perceived more as helpful protectors rather than as brutal adversaries. But law enforcement is necessarily dangerous and often violent, and the people who are attracted to such work are more likely to be tough rather than tenderhearted. Exertion of power, the legal authority to use force, can be very exciting. Thus "clout" is a kind of fringe benefit for some types of individuals, compensating perhaps for the low pay and unpleasant working conditions. But if this enjoyment in the use of force becomes a dominant motivation, it can result in unnecessary violence and a public with legitimate complaints of police brutality. One way to minimize this problem would be to provide special incentives for the enlistment of people with different kinds of motivations, as noted below.

Most judges, social workers, and parole officers view the criminal control problem quite differently than do the police who must risk their lives to arrest the criminals. All concerned would benefit if every judge, every parole officer, and every prison official were forced to serve at least one year as an ordinary police officer. In fact, such service on the police force should be a prerequisite requirement for holding any other position in the Criminal Justice System. Personal experience with the problem of crime when it is being committed would counteract the "ivory tower" philosophy which presently permeates the system.

The idea is not to limit these other offices to the type of people normally found in the average police force. The idea is to force those who have ambitions for these higher paid jobs to serve a period of apprenticeship, to learn the job from the ground up, as the saying goes. If this could be accomplished, the police force itself would also be upgraded by the presence of men of high intelligence, ambition, and education. Thus the police image would be improved at the same time that the future decision makers would be improving their grasp on reality.

Implementation of this proposal would necessarily require a "grandfather clause" exempting current incumbents from this service requirement. The requirement would be for all future candidates after some cutoff date which would give enough time for future candidates to get in their service requirement.

The Screamer

The scream for help is the oldest method of passive defense. In simpler societies, those who rushed to help the victim were not harassed by the endless confusion, complexities, inanities, and liabilities of what passes for justice today. In those societies the scream for help was so effective that women and children were reasonably safe, even in bad neighborhoods, as long as numbers of people were present. Today, however, most people are well aware of the price associated with "becoming involved," and the scream for help falls on deaf ears.

Putting policemen back on the walking beat would be a step in the right direction, but the policeman cannot be everywhere at once. What is needed is the ability to hear a scream, right in the police station, regardless of wherever and whenever the scream occurs.

This effect could be accomplished by mass production of an electronic screamer which would be a cheap, high power, short life, radio transmitter about the size of a roll of dimes, actuated by a hand squeeze or a thumb button.

Once actuated, it could not be turned off until the batteries run down, which would take at least several minutes.

Each screamer would be numbered and registered with the police, to prevent malicious false alarms. Each screamer would be encased in alloy steel, so that even if the criminal discovers it, he cannot destroy it before it has alerted the police.

Each police substation would have suitable direction finding equipment, with auxiliary stations for the necessary triangulation. The station would be always listening, and able to instantly fix the position of the scream. Thus, any time an assault is impending, the owner of the screamer can silently call for help and have it arrive in time to do some good.

Such a device would probably cost less than $25, perhaps even less than $10. Everyone who is worried about their safety would buy them, and crimes of violence on the street would be significantly reduced.

Assuming that such a device is marketed and bought by considerable numbers of people, the newspapers would soon carry stories about crimes thwarted, or criminals caught, or frightened off, by this device. Undoubtedly there would be a market for dummy screamers, costing less than a dollar, but which would appear to be identical to the real thing. These also would be effective since the crook could not, in most cases, afford to call the bluff by waiting around to see if the police really come, especially if the police make a practice of not turning on their sirens.

The device described above is the low cost, mass production version. Rich people, who have to be exposed to dangerous neighborhoods, might provide a market for more sophisticated screamers which would provide voice and sound communication input to the police tape recorder during the real time incident. Eventually some of these might include two way transceiver communication, still on the basis of one shot emergency actuation. Of course, all of these devices would have provisions for recharging and resetting for reuse, but this would only be possible by a special key which would not normally be carried on the person carrying the screamer.

It is the current practice of certain progressive police departments to exploit the existing two way radio communication system of taxicabs and delivery vehicles as means of reporting crime in process, or of dangerous situations developing. Two way hand screamers would extend this capability for a much broader coverage.

Thus by using this simple device, based entirely on existing technology, we could reduce muggings, rapes, street robbery, and gang fights to negligible proportions, assuming the courts would dispense justice to the larger number of crooks arrested.

Reverence for Life

The primary purpose of law is to prevent fraud and violence. However, to accomplish this task, the police must have the power of applying whatever degree of force that is necessary to enforce the law. With a law-abiding public, this may involve nothing more violent than a traffic ticket. Other situations, where the offender resists arrest and attempts either to flee or to assault the police, will require additional force. If the police officer is big and strong, and has a good working knowledge of judo and karate, he may be able to subdue his suspect without the use of any weapon at all. But if the criminal is also big and strong and also has a good working knowledge of judo and karate, the policeman will need some sort of weapon if he is to come out ahead in the fight.

Of course the criminal may also have various kinds of weapons, so there is no question but that a policeman needs to carry a handgun and know how and when to use it. He also needs his night stick for the in-between situations where the club is enough force and there is no valid reason to endanger life by the use of a firearm.

While these two weapons have been the basic equipment for many years, it is clear that they are quite inadequate for many situations. One situation is where the policeman attempts to question a suspect whom he believes to be armed and dangerous. In reality, the suspect may be unarmed and perfectly harmless, and may, in fact, be guilty of some other minor offense, perhaps a petty larceny, or littering, etc. The suspect may decide to break away and flee, in the belief that he can outrun the policeman. In this situation, the policeman may feel justified in drawing his revolver and shooting the fleeing "murderer." The next day's paper then reports the unfortunate death of a young litterbug, or a bicycle thief; another victim of "police brutality."

Another common situation is where the policeman is attempting to subdue a suspect who is frantically resisting arrest, to such an extent that the officer feels justified in using his club. Then the result is a gory scene for the news reporters or the TV. This produces instant sympathy for the offender and hatred for the police. Perhaps the onlookers and the suspect resisting arrest happen to be of a different race than that of the policeman. The sight of blood and the spectacle of a big cop beating up on one of the neighborhood boys may well incite the crowd to attack the policeman and the whole thing can thus escalate into a race riot. It has happened many times in the past and it will certainly happen many times in the future.

Still another situation is the politically inspired riot situation where the agitators are deliberately attempting to provoke the police into a club wielding assault, or to get a few innocent people killed by trigger happy police or national guardsmen. Or perhaps it is a civil disobedience demonstration, with masses of passive protesters sitting down in the streets or blocking traffic. A really well organized riot will have the passive protesters blocking the streets so that the firemen and the squad cars cannot get to the place where they are burning the town down.

The police have tried a number of counter weapons and tactics to overcome these various types of situations. Tear gas, fire hoses, rubber bullets, and massive mobile manpower all have proven value, but these weapons cannot be carried by individual patrolmen; they are suitable only to a large-scale disturbance which can be foreseen far enough ahead for the equipment to be readied and the tactical plans prepared. What about the spontaneous situations, how can we equip the patrolman so that he can handle a wider variety of dangerous situations without killing people with his gun?

Actually, nearly every arrest involves some sequence in which the suspect may have a very good chance of escaping if he is fleet of foot and if the policeman is reluctant to draw his gun and shoot. Perhaps what is needed is a second, non-lethal gun which can immobilize without killing. If such a weapon were available, the policeman would be able to prevent the escape of a suspect without killing him or risking a heart attack in a cross-country race. In fact, there are very few situations where a non-lethal gun would not work just as well as a lethal gun. Even in situations where the officer is in danger of physical attack, a non-lethal gun could be decisive if the tranquilizing action were fast enough. There are many problems involved in bringing this idea to reality—what kind of gun, how to obtain a safe but effective dose for different-sized people, how to avoid injury to vital areas of the body. It is not an easy problem, and it is probably not possible to make such a weapon perfectly safe. But it would be a lot safer than getting leadpoisoning from .45 caliber slugs!

In addition to the technical advantages involved, there is a very subtle but important psychological benefit. There is a very significant difference in the image of a policeman as one who kills because he cannot catch and one who arrests, when arrest is necessary, but with respect for the basic right to life of even a fleeing criminal. Our objective, psychologically, should be to achieve the police-community relationship which has been traditional in England where the police did not even need to carry guns at all and yet, with the aid of the people of the community and sensible judges, they were quite successful in keeping the streets relatively safe and free from crime.

Qualifications for Judges

Every job has qualifications, explicit or implicit, written or unwritten. There also seems to be some sort of Parkinson's Law which operates such that the more important the job, the harder it is to measure performance or to define meaningful qualifications. Where the performance is highly visible to the electorate, such as the mayoralty or the presidency, the democratic process assures some relationship between qualifications and election. However, this does not work so well in the election of judges.

In the fight against crime, there is no office more important than that held by the judge. Yet an examination of the process by which a man is selected for this office shows that it has little if any relationship to the effectiveness with which the man will operate to protect the innocent, punish the guilty, and deter future crime.

Historically, judges are elected as part of a party slate. Since their performance is unpublicized, knowledge of their capability is effectively restricted to that small percent of the population with which they interface, ie, criminal offenders, criminal lawyers, and other parties with direct financial interests in the results of their decisions. Their ultimate customer, the ordinary law abiding citizen, has no data to form any meaningful independent judgment. Since the voters lack information, the democratic process breaks down.

The resulting debacle in performance has led to attempts at reform by abandoning the democratic process under the slogan of "Let's eliminate politics from the selection of judges." Sometimes these attempts result in real improvement and sometimes they make matters worse. For instance the sitting judge principle, whereby opposing candidacies are discouraged, does protect a competent judge from attack by political opportunists. However it also shields an incompetent from the normal results of poor performance on the job.

Another approach is preselection by a "nonpartisan" board of experts, who select several names which are then certified either for appointment by the governor, or for listing on the ballot. Here again, the question boils down to who selects the selection board, and what criteria is truly controlling the selection. In the end, most judges are selected primarily because of political acceptability, not with the electorate at large, but with the infra-structure of the major political parties. Unfortunately there is a heavy influence exerted by organized crime, and by business interests which may be affected by the decisions of each particular judge.

What we really need are some criteria by which a judge's performance may be related to their ultimate responsibility of protecting the innocent and deterring crime at a reasonable cost in time and dollars. If some generally acceptable criteria could be established, then an orderly mode of advancement might be possible with judges aspiring to higher positions on the basis of established superior performance, rather than on the basis of political indebtedness. If such a criteria were published prior to election day, then the democratic process might again be effective, since the voters could "keep score" and compare the relative performance of competing candidates on a realistic basis.

From the point of view of cost to the taxpayer, a judge's performance might be described by statistics such as:

1. Average hours per week on the bench.
2. Cases completed per year (weighted by category).
3. Taxpayer cost per case.
4. Average time for each case, including delays and continuances.

However, this gives only part of the story. In addition to cost there is judicial effectiveness. This might be measured by statistics such as:

1. Percent of cases reversed by appeal to a higher court.
2. Percent of cases where the accused commits another offence of equal or greater magnitude.
3. Relative crime rate in his jurisdiction as compared to the average rate for similar jurisdictions.

Modern computers can handle purely statistical data with ease. Using the computer, the FBI could easily keep books on every judge and publish the data several months in advance of each election. This type of information could then become the means for enabling voters to choose judges on a basis of performance rather than on a basis of political party affiliation.

In addition to providing comparative data, so that the better man will have a better chance for selection, there should also be minimum qualifications so that those who are totally incompetent could not qualify, regardless of their political popularity. The idea here is not necessarily to obtain the best, it is to eliminate the worst. Since experience is of major importance in developing wisdom, one of the minimum qualifications for holding high judicial office ought to be simply that of experience in performance of a similar job in a lower office. Thus it ought to be an across-the-board requirement that Supreme Court appointees must have served several years on a lower court of appeal, and that Appellate Court candidates must have had several years of service on a court of original jurisdiction. This one principle would wipe out a great portion of the present confusion that exists today due to the use of the United States Supreme Court as political patronage for men who have no judicial experience. Congress has the Constitutional authority for accomplishing this reform, and this should have priority if there is to be any progress in combating crime. It is foolish to complain about decisions made by inexperienced judges when there is such an obvious means for improving the situation.

Predictable Justice

Few people are willing to put their hand on a hot stove more than once. In this case the predictability factor is 100%. On the other hand, 50,000 people are killed each year by autos, and approximately 300,000 are killed each year by cigarettes, if we are to believe the statistics. In these cases the predictability factor is very small, with probabilities of less than .1% for the punishment for any particular offense. Thus people will take chances with autos and cigarettes which kill them, but not with hot stoves, which merely hurt their hands for a short period of time. The glamour and excitement of doing dangerous things disappears when the punishment changes from an unknown to a known, from an improbability to a certainty.

The attractiveness of crime is directly related to the estimation of the improbability of being punished. First, there is the probability of not getting caught, for any particular offense. On top of this, there is the probability of not being convicted even if arrested, or of getting off with a suspended sentence even if convicted. Even if sentenced, there is the chance of getting a short sentence, or an early parole for compliant behavior. And there is always the hope of pardon from the governor or by way of the latest decision of the Supreme Court. In addition to all of this, there may be a complete lack of knowledge of how bad the punishment might actually be in case things turn out for the worst.

The average offender is not a probability expert, and even if he were, he would have an impossible problem in trying to assess the true chances of paying the penalty for his crime. Therefore, he gives up the attempt and simply disregards the possibility of punishment, except perhaps for taking obvious measures to reduce the probability of getting caught. (An important exception to this conclusion is the case with organized crime, where adequate provisions are made to reduce the probability of punishment even when the offender is caught.)

As a result of this uncertainty, the severity of the punishment becomes ineffective as a deterrent, since the offender judges the overall probability of full punishment to be negligible. This situation accounts for the misleading statement that, "Studies show that the severity of punishment has no measurable effect in deterring crime." Any effective deterrent requires that the potential offender fear the punishment, and believe that the probability of its occurrence is high enough such the consequences cannot be ignored.

If we are to make progress in fighting crime, we must recognize that the predictability of punishment is as important as the punishment itself. Anything that will convince the potential offender that there is a real penalty awaiting him will have a direct effect in reducing crime. One way to improve predictability would be to specify the exact punishment for every conceivable crime, and make this list available to those who are planning their next "job."

Precedent for this approach exists. For instance, in the Book of Deuteronomy there is a long list of offenses covering harlotry, rape, sodomy, loan sharking, etc., and for each offense there is a definite punishment. In that system the punishment is related approximately to the seriousness of the crime.

However, the idea of exact apportionment of punishment to the degree of the offense can be carried too far, and in a non-computer society, it becomes impossible to list a "fair" punishment that will be applicable for every case falling in that category. Because of this there has been a tendency to specify wide limits of punishment, and leave it up to the judge to fit the punishment to the particular circumstances in each case. This, of course, destroys the predictability since the actual punishment depends on which judge you get, and how he feels on the day he pronounces the sentence.

Today we have the computer, and we can make good use of it to solve this problem. The solution would be to program the computer such that when any particular crime is specified, and when the circumstances are also properly specified, the computer will instantly print out a description of the average punishment meted out for that crime and those circumstances.

The input provided to the computer would consist of factors such as:

1. Type of offense.
2. Type of evidence (confession, eyewitness, circumstance, etc.).
3. Estimated residual probability of innocence.
4. Personal data.
5. Past offenses.
6. Motivations producing this offense.
7. Degree of organization (individual, partner, gang, mob).
8. "Unnecessary" violence.
9. "Unnecessary" property damage.
10. Weapons employed.
11. Weapons carried.
12. Prearrest repentance and restitution.

13. Post arrest cooperation concerning other criminal offenses

With this input information, the computer would instantly print out data useful in determining the sentence, such as:

1. Legal description of the offense.
2. Legal limits of the severity of punishment.
3. Statistics on frequency and trend of this type offense.
4. Average severity of punishment, modified by individual case factors.
5. Weighting values used for each modifying factor.
6. Alternate equivalent punishments.
7. Sentence reduction recommended for future cooperation such as information, restitution, witnessing, etc.

Using such a system, the judge would have an assistant punch an input card in accordance with the facts of the case as determined. Using a remote access time sharing computer facility, the judge would get an immediate print out of the previously described statistical information. This would tell him the whole story on precedent and current practice, and give him a recommended severity of sentence for the case as he has ascertained it.

Of course, the judge is not obligated to use the recommendation as furnished. There may be some unusual circumstances not covered by the input card, or the judge may simply disagree with the other judges, and may specify either a more or less severe sentence. In any case, the judge would record his decision and the reason for modifying the recommended sentence, and this information would also be fed back into the computer. The decision itself would end up influencing the value of the mean severity of punishment, and any disagreement as to the importance of some weighting factor would also be used to compute a modified weighting factor for that particular circumstance. Thus the program would be continually updated, giving an accurate picture of the current expected punishment for every conceivable crime and circumstance.

An essential part of such a system is the fact that anyone, including the potential criminal himself, can get a print-out for a hypothetical crime, including the modifications caused by varying circumstances. For instance, he might learn that the penalty for robbing a gas station is one year, whereas if bodily injury is inflicted, the penalty is five years, and if a gun is used the penalty is ten years. Using this information, he may decide not to carry a gun, and if discovered, he may flee rather than attack. Of course there is always the possibility that he may conclude that it really isn't worth the risk anyway, and decide not to commit the crime.

It may be observed that there is a possibility that criminals might find out that some crimes really do pay, in that the punishment is so light that it makes sense to commit the crime. An analogy is the situation where the parking lot costs $1.50, but a parking ticket costs only $1.00. The predictable result is a sharp increase in the number of parking tickets. The solution in such cases is to increase the severity of the punishment to the point where the potential offenders conclude that the rewards do not justify the risk.

Several decisions must be made as a part of establishing such a computer system. For instance, if several punishments are available, what constitutes equivalence? Is a month in solitary confinement equal to a year at hard labor, or to three years of penal "rehabilitation"? Is a fine of $100 the same for a rich man as for a poor man? How can these different things be reduced to provide an equivalent, or at least a reasonably equivalent deterrent?

Although these decisions are hard, they are necessary

and they are made on a casual intuitive basis every time a judge pronounces sentence. With the computer system, these decisions would become predictable and much of the uncertainty would disappear. There may also be some important side benefits in that equivalent punishments may permit the selection of the lowest cost method for obtaining the same end result. If one month of solitary confinement is approximately equivalent in value to three years of ordinary imprisonment, then there is an opportunity here for a 97% cost reduction!

Organized Crime

A proper analysis of organized crime would fill a volume much larger than this book. Generating a practical solution that will solve the problem or even provide significant alleviation seems almost a hopeless task. However, there are two or three measures which could be taken and which could be expected to produce some improvement. These include passage of legislation which would more clearly define the organization for criminal purposes as a crime in and of itself, a campaign directed at the criminal "workers" instead of the bosses, and a sophisticated approach to the basic problem of what constitutes optimum strategy in minimizing vice and corruption. It is assumed without further discussion that the police will be able to work with a reformed court and will not be handcuffed by the present arbitrary policies which tend to prevent electronic surveillance, and the use of certified recordings as evidence.

The strategy of society for coping with crime is primarily and historically based on providing sufficient deterrence so that "Crime Doesn't Pay," along with a reliance on social, moral, and religious pressures which produce unpleasant feelings when we do evil, and which produce pleasant feelings when we do good. Organized crime represents a successful adaptation which nullifies both of these strategies. For organized crime, it pays exceedingly well. There is also a subculture, a code, a philosophy that obtains primary allegiance, and which substitutes loyalty to the Mafia in place of the normal identification with society. The true mobster gets pleasant feelings from his crimes.

If it is agreed that the ordinary laws and punishments are incapable of coping with organized crime, it necessarily follows that special laws and punishments are required before any progress can be expected. Suppose for instance, that the FBI were to be given blanket authority to arrest, interrogate, drug, hypnotize, torture and execute anyone that they decided was affiliated with the Mafia. The Mafia would be out of business in a few weeks. However a free society is very loath to create such a police force since history abounds with examples where the unlimited power of the police results in a totalitarian dictatorship and the destruction of everyone's freedom.

The real problem is to define the minimum change required, the least increase in police authority which would be sufficient to tip the balance against organized crime. An interesting proposal by a former member of the Mafia was to simply pass a law against organized crime as such. Making the fact of organizing for criminal purposes an offense with mandatory punishments of great severity, could provide the necessary margin for success. Thus offenses such as gambling, attempted extortion, usury, attempted bribery, which would normally carry light sentences, would automatically involve an additional ten or twenty years at hard labor without parole, if done by direction of a boss, or as part of an organized enterprise.

Once armed with this weapon, the honest police forces would be in a position to implement the second suggestion, that of a frontal attack on the "workers" who actually commit the acts of violence, rather than on the bosses, who merely plan and give orders. The objective here is to destroy the organization by attrition from the bottom up, rather than from the top down. With massive arrests of the workers, the bosses must either abandon legal support for many of their workers and let them go to jail, or restrict operations. If the workers are abandoned, many will defect to cooperate with the police for reduction in sentence, and many others will leave town for other employment. Thus the net effect would be a constriction of operations and an overall reduction in the power and profit of organized crime.

The opposite strategy of going for Mr. Big is futile. Suppose after much effort and time, Mr. Big is finally convicted. He either continues to direct the operation from his jail cell, or another Mr. Big takes over. If there is competition for the job, the net result is a sharp increase in the murder rate until the issue is settled. A cynic may observe that this doesn't matter since the crooks are murdering each other, but this is hardly the way to combat organized crime. Any time the government abandons its monopoly of the use of coercive force, the people are in for big trouble.

The main source of the strength of organized crime is the fervent insistence by the poor and the uneducated of their right to gamble, and the equally fervent insistence by the upper classes that they shall not be permitted to waste their money that way. Those who are prosperous have no difficulty in finding legal ways to gamble, whether it be in the stock market, the commodities market, real estate speculation, or simply trips to the track, or Las Vegas. If it is all right for the rich to gamble, why isn't it all right for the poor?

If we eliminate the veneer and look at the basic situation, it ought to be perfectly clear that the poor and the uneducated should not gamble because they cannot afford to lose. However, the poor and uneducated are generally unable to recognize the futility of gambling when the odds are stacked against them. In a truly laissez faire society, it would be none of the business of the upper classes to decide whether or not the free citizens of the lower classes become further impoverished by gambling. However it is equally clear that in a semi-welfare society, society as a whole starts paying when any individual becomes impoverished. It doesn't really make much sense to permit a welfare recipient to gamble away funds provided for his support by the taxpayer.

Incidentally, this point invalidates all efforts by the state to use gambling profits to finance education or otherwise provide social benefits for those who are supposedly unable to afford additional taxes. Gambling is an exceedingly vicious and regressive tax, since it is paid only by those who cannot understand their own exploitation. Those who can afford it the least pay the most.

If society were really divided neatly into the upper and lower classes, this apparent conflict of interest might appear unreconcilable. However, the fact is that there are many people who want to gamble, and who really could absorb a considerable drop in their own standard of living without becoming welfare recipients. If we believe in freedom, we should be prepared to treat these people as responsible adults and let them decide for themselves whether to gamble or not. Welfare recipients are in a different class, and there is no reason why they should be permitted to spend the taxpayers cash for the futile excitement of gambling against the odds.

If gambling were to be legalized, it should be done in such a fashion that gambling on credit, or using welfare funds would be extremely difficult if not impossible. If gambling were legalized without such provisions, organized crime would be the beneficiary, since they operate the loan shark business which exploits those who are willing to gamble, but who cannot afford to pay the losses without committing crime to obtain the money.

Thus, a sophisticated policy would be required. Professional gamblers, bookies, etc., would be licensed by the government and would pay a stiff yearly rental for the privilege. The total number of operations would be limited so as to prevent mass merchandizing of gambling services. The easiest and most logical way to ration out the licenses would be to set the fee quite high, up to the point where a few vacancies would exist. This would avoid some of the abuses in granting, transferring, or refusing gambling licenses.

In addition to being licensed, the professional gamblers would be responsible for restricting their services to those who are financially solvent and would require disclosure of assets and income, and liabilities as a prerequisite for accepting a customer. Part of the deal would be submission of reports on the amounts won and lost by their customers for federal income tax purposes. Another requirement would be that full information of the actual odds must be furnished to every customer and displayed at every establishment. In addition to all of this, the government would impose a tax on the net profits, equivalent to the ordinary corporation tax, and would require full accounting to verify the returns. Under such a system, the gambling business would be as controlled and taxed as every other business, or perhaps a little more so since they would probably be prevented from aggressive merchandizing operations such as advertisements in the mass media, or lobbying for preferred legislation.

If such a controlled system were possible, it could provide a major blow to the continued existence of organized crime, since gambling and loan sharking are the mob's bread and butter. Without the financial power provided by these "businesses" the ability of the mob to operate in other business areas would also suffer some attrition.

Does Parole Really Help?

Parole is the procedure by which the court allows the convicted offender to go free after serving only a portion of his sentence, and as long as he is not caught in a new crime. The granting of parole is usually based on the convict's attitude, behavior, and his subservience to the authority of the correctional establishment. Since it costs about one tenth as much to keep a man on parole as compared to keeping him in prison, this low cost is often cited as one of the major advantages of this procedure.

Another cited advantage is that parole offers a means for the establishment to exercise some degree of control over the offender, and this should reduce the expectation that he will go back to a life of crime immediately after his release. Most prisoners are very anxious to be released on parole. Since the granting of parole is a discretionary act on the part of the correctional establishment, the establishment treasures this power over the liberty of its charges, and uses it as a means for obtaining subservience to its rehabilitation policies and programs.

However when measured against the requirements needed for a low cost deterrent against crime, parole may have more disadvantages than advantages. The records show that about 40% of the convicted offenders on parole are unsuccessful in that their parole is revoked for cause. Sometimes this cause is simply carelessness in not following the rules for reporting. About half the time however, it is associated with an arrest for the commission of additional crimes. So the important question is whether or not this 40% revocation represents success in terms of any net benefit to society.

Currently fashionable doctrine argues that this 40% revocation does indeed represent a net benefit to society since after all, 60% of the paroles are "successes." This argument seems plausible until one examines what is really meant by "success." In most cases, success means the offender didn't get caught in a period of two or three years, it doesn't mean that he is no longer committing crimes. The FBI reports that only 75% of the reported crimes against persons such as assault, rape, manslaughter and murder are cleared by arrest of a suspect, and only 20% of the reported crimes against property. Other surveys show that the actual crime is about three times higher that the reported crime. Thus it is clear that on the average, a parolee will be committing about ten additional crimes before he is caught and his parole record is changed from "successful" to "unsuccessful."

However the most serious defect in the parole concept is that it nullifies the whole idea of unavoidable punishment for criminal offence, and thus destroys the basis for justice and deterrence. In order for there to be any deterrence at all, there must be a credible link between the crime as a cause, and the punishment as the effect.

The reason why no one voluntarily puts his hand on a red hot stove twice is that the "punishment" is perceived as being the direct and unavoidable result of the "crime." If we didn't feel the burn until a year later, and then only 5% of the time, and then only if we couldn't talk the judge or the parole officer into something less hurtful than the normally expected burn, people would be leaning on hot stoves all the time!

The parole idea also destroys the basis for any sincere rehabilitation. If the criminal understands that the punishment he gets is the automatic result of the crime he has committed, then he has no one to blame but himself for the dire consequences. But if the punishment is actually the result of evaluative judgments by a parole board or officer, he will quite rightly conclude that he is being punished because certain people want to punish him, and not as any automatic consequence of his own decisions or actions. The result is that the offender will blame others rather than himself, and thereby prevent even the first step toward rehabilitation, which is the recognition that he is wrong and needs to change.

Not only does it prevent the self evaluation needed for reform, it actually increases his hatred and resentment against society. It does this by destroying the man's inherent integrity and dignity by forcing him to pretend a subservience and cooperation that he does not really feel, in order to convince the establishment that he is ready for parole. They force him to grovel! If he proudly refuses to put on the act that they require, he just doesn't get the parole. So he grovels, but inwardly he is being filled with a long lasting rage and hatred, and a desire for revenge on a system that is not content with taking his freedom, but seeks to manipulate his soul as well. Thus the parole system favors those who find it easy to put on an act, and it discriminates against those who are prevented from such debasement by their own inner self respect.

Liberty is a very precious human right, and a man's liberty should not be at the discretion of any other man, except as narrowly prescribed by law. Parole puts men in a master-slave relationship and so violates this basic principle. Since it does not prevent the parolee from committing additional crimes, and since it prevents both rehabilitation and deterrence, we should seek some other method for coping with the high cost of administrating punishment. We ought to be able to find a better way.

The Rights of Prisoners

Recently the public has become more aware of the unbelievable abuses that go on daily in our prisons and jails. One abuse which surfaces often enough to indicate its common occurrence is the practice of allowing the inmates to band together for the purpose of homosexual gang rape of new inmates.

If the new arrival is big enough and strong enough, he might be able to put up enough of a fight to win some degree of safety. If he is a member of a well organized gang which has a number of members in that particular prison, he might be saved by the intervention of his friends. If he has some way of getting money, he may be able to pay off the leaders of the homosexuals, at least for a period of time. But often the only way to avoid repeated gang rape is to "get married" to some dominant homosexual and depend on him for protection.

A similar abuse occurs when a child or youth who may be arrested for nothing more serious than running away from home is thrown into jail with an older, hardened, homosexual criminal. The guard goes away and the child is brutalized in an unbelievable manner with no one to save him.

It is hard to explain how the public, composed of generally law abiding people, can tolerate such conditions. Perhaps it is because they cannot really believe how bad the conditions are. Perhaps they have never considered how perverted caged criminals can become when they are denied normal sexual outlets but are presented with abundant opportunity to engage in homosexual activity without restraint from the law.

When the officials in charge are asked why such conditions are allowed to persist, they cover up by pretending that the conditions are not really so bad; it just happens once in awhile, and there isn't anything that can be done about it, anyway. When proof is offered that it is indeed a common occurrence, the officials fall back on their favorite theme, which is that they do not have enough money to provide adequate guard service. "If only there were more money in the budget such conditions would doubtless be alleviated." Another excuse is that it is too dangerous for the guards to stay with the prisoners all the time, and so such activities must be accepted as a normal part of prison life.

Those who make such excuses should be fired immediately. The only proper response to evidence of such conditions is that the problem will be immediately corrected, by whatever measures that may be required. For instance, if necessary, each prisoner can be physically restrained by chains and handcuffs so that it would be impossible to attack a fellow prisoner.

There is a very fundamental point here, and that is

that punishment authorized by law must be applied by lawfully authorized personnel. When the "Correctional" institution accepts custody of a man it also accepts the responsibility to protect that man from assault by other prisoners, or by non-prisoners for that matter. Allowing prisoners to attack each other and to enslave other weaker prisoners is a blatant violation of basic human rights as well as a gross violation of the Constitutional prohibition against cruel and unusual punishment.

Every purpose of the correctional system, whether it is rehabilitation, isolation, deterrence, or simple vengence, every purpose is thwarted when the agents of the government allow the control of prisoners to slip out of their hands. Punishment, to do any good at all, must be measured and authorized by law. Therefore, all punishment suffered by a prisoner which is not authorized by law but which happens because of negligence by those in charge constitutes a crime, and if justice were really to be served, every warden who knowingly permits such conditions should be tried and convicted, sentenced, and punished the same as if he himself were caught raping a small boy in the park.

Of course, homosexual rape is not the only reason for interprisoner attacks. It may be for other reasons such as racial hatred in an "integrated" prison; it may be because a gang of terrorists such as the Black Panthers are "organizing" the men for a riot; or it may be a simple matter of extortion of money by physical violence. When we consider that in prison we have an unnatural concentration of violent, ruthless men who are sexually frustrated and who have nothing to do to alleviate their frustrations, it ought to be obvious that there will be no peace in prison if the prisoners are allowed to have close contact with each other. The only way to avoid assaults therefore, is to keep them separate from each other so that they will not have any opportunity to attack.

As mentioned in another section, if we would substitute a short term of solitary confinement for a protracted period of ordinary penal servitude, we could make the deterrent more vivid for the same equivalent punishment, and also reduce the cost by more than 90%. It would also entirely eliminate all interprisoner attacks and thus solve this particular problem. However, until such overall improvement is accepted and put into practice, each warden must face up to his responsibility for the safety of his prisoners by providing sufficient segregation so as to keep those who are likely to attack away from those who are likely to be attacked.

Since the present establishment in charge of our prisons are obviously corrupted to the point where they cannot see any serious problem here, it will be up to the people to force their government to take the leadership in correcting this problem. The Legislature of each State should define mandatory procedures and requirements for the handling, transportation, and "storage" of live human beings which will protect them from criminal attack while in the custody of the State, and the Governor should make sure that such procedures are enforced.

As a minimum, prisoners should be physically separated such that attack or coercion is impossible whenever they are not under the direct observation and control of guards. Each prisoner should have a separate cell, or at least have the right to choose or reject their cell mate without coercion. When separation is not possible and observation is impractical as, for instance, when transporting prisoners in a van, each prisoner should be restrained by manacles or other devices so that attack is impossible.

Those who are known to have motives for attack, whether such motives are sexual, racial, or personal, should be totally segregated from those who are likely to be their victims. Identified homosexuals should not be allowed to associate with nonhomosexuals but should be kept completely separate, preferably in separate institutions.

All of these procedures should be documented in writing, concisely and simply enough so that the prisoners themselves will understand what are their rights. The regulations should be specific, and in sufficient detail to cover all normal situations. Such procedures should be enforced by regular and surprise inspections and by removal of prisoners from the institution for secret interrogation by commissioners who have no organizational relationship to the prison administration, and by members of the press. Any prison official found in noncompliance should be automatically dismissed after a first warning.

If sufficient public pressure cannot be focused to obtain action from the Governor, then an alternate remedy would be to bring criminal charges against the warden of an offending institution. If a test case could be filed with sufficient evidence to jeopardize the reputation, career, and possibly the freedom of an offending warden, the resulting publicity would doubtless result in the filing of other cases and thus enough public attention would be focused to achieve reform.

A society which cannot even protect the safety of those who are in its custody cannot possibly begin to provide adequate protection for the general public. It is hard to see how such a society can survive. What a mockery our "correctional" institutions have become!

Corrected Corrections

Since the greatest failure of our criminal justice system is in the area of "Corrections," this area also offers the greatest opportunity for improvement, once the basic cause of the failure is understood. However it will require a traumatic change, involving a total abandonment of presently fashionable concepts, and a willingness to admit gross error in concept as well as in performance. This is another way of saying that a meaningful reform will have to be imposed from the outside, since the "experts" presently in control of these institutions cannot be expected to initiate the total change that is required.

If one should ask the purpose of police, courts, prisons, penitentiaries, parole boards, etc., he could get a variety of answers including concepts such as deterrence, isolation, and rehabilitation. From a functional point of view, each of these concepts is associated with an entirely different purpose. Thus, the purpose of deterrence is to nullify the incentives which motivate men to commit crime. It is intended to cause them to refrain because of fear of the consequences. The purpose of isolation is simply to remove dangerous individuals from the general society in order to physically restrain them from repeated offenses. The purpose of rehabilitation is to change the inner motivation patterns so that a man will decide voluntarily that he wants to go straight rather than crooked.

The odd thing is that we seem to expect one institution to accomplish all of these purposes, each of which are in direct conflict with the other. Of course, what really happens is that we choose sides and root for our own pet objective. Thus anyone who really believes in the correctional function, will automatically downgrade the deterrent function and the isolation function. Similarly, we find other people who believe in deterrence and they have plans for improving this function, at the expense, naturally, of the other functions. And so it goes.

One point must be established, and that is that no one institution can accomplish all of these mutually conflicting objectives. Deterrence requires the creation of fear, and fear requires unpleasant treatment. On the other hand, rehabilitation requires love, trust, and cooperation and this cannot be imposed by force of punishment, or by fear, or by unpleasant treatment. Similarly the present system for the isolation of dangerous individuals conflicts with the basic objectives of both deterrence and rehabilitation.

If this one point can be established, then the answer becomes obvious. We must provide a distinctively different institution for each separate objective, and let each separate institution exert its efforts and develop its methods to assure success in pursuit of its single objective. Thus in this concept, there would be a separate institution for rehabilitation and it would be totally unconnected with any institution for punishment. There would also be an institution for deterrence which would have no other objective than to provide a fear of punishment so as to deter other potential offenders and inhibit any repetition of offense. Similarly there would be an institution which would not be concerned with either punishment or rehabilitation, but would merely provide physical separation and sufficient surveillance as needed to prevent dangerous individuals from harming themselves or others.

It is necessary to fix each function in its proper place in the time sequence so that it will have the best chance of success. In this connection, it is suggested that deterrence be applied first, and that the degree of deterrence be escalated with repeated offenses. If the deterrence job is properly accomplished, the first offender will learn absolutely nothing during his punishment except that it was quite unpleasant, and will be considerably worse if he comes back a second or third time. It is to be expected that the convict will *hate* the deterrence institution and this feeling can be useful if it reinforces his desire never to return.

If deterrence is to be effective, the memory of the punishment should be vivid rather than obscure. Thus a comparatively short period spent in solitary confinement should be equivalent to a much longer period spent in the ordinary routine of prison life. If this holds true, it follows that the deterrence institution should make maximum use of solitary confinement, with a suitable reduction in the sentence time to equalize the overall severity of the punishment.

In addition to making the deterrent easier to remember, solitary confinement has other important advantages. For one thing, it would eliminate the sexual assaults and gang rapes by aggressive sodomites which in many prisons provides the new inmate with his first initiation into the realities of prison life. It would also prevent the formation of alliances and partnerships for future criminal activity. It would avoid the situation where older and more experienced criminals educate the first offender on how to commit crime with less chance of getting caught. And last and most important, it would prevent the development of criminal psychology and identification in the mind of the first offender which then becomes the chief barrier to future rehabilitation.

Since the convict will bitterly hate the deterrence institution, the rehabilitation institution must be totally separate from the deterrence institution in fact as well as in appearance. This implies that the rehabilitation function cannot be controlled or even financed by the government. It must be performed by private charitable organizations such as the Red Cross or the Salvation Army or various churches, etc. The only connection between the two classes of institutions would be the requirement that the release date and time be publicly advertised so that the private agencies would have a chance to contact the convict as he emerges from the place of punishment.

It will be observed that the people who are emotionally identified with rehabilitation, will be the ones who will staff the private agency. Thus the convict will find sincere sympathy for his tale of woe. His counselor will really and truly be "on his side." He is smart enough to detect insincerity, so this situation is what is really required if he is to have any chance for rehabilitation. If he accepts the offer of aid and guidance, he is halfway on the road to a real change of inner attitude, which of course is just another way of describing the rehabilitation process.

Thus, those who commit offenses will have the benefit both of deterrence and the opportunity for voluntary rehabilitation, at a time and in a manner which will prevent mutual nullification. However, for some, this will not work and they will repeat and suffer the escalated punishment. For those who continue after the third or fourth offense, it becomes obvious that neither the deterrence nor the opportunity for rehabilitation are doing the job. Thus society must turn to its last ditch defense which is to isolate the chronic offender at the least cost to the taxpayer. At this point there is no real purpose in either punishment or rehabilitation, so there should be no more punishment than absolutely required to prevent him from being a menace to his fellow prisoners, or to himself.

The suggestion here is to establish a controlled city which might be called "Vacationland." Vacationland would be just like any other city except that it has a guarded perimeter, controlled access, and in addition, all inhabitants are under constant surveillance by a variety of electronic devices, and by the inhabitants themselves. Every action requires permission, and every movement a sign in and sign out, as with any other security area. Each inhabitant is assigned to a counselor, who is responsible for keeping him out of trouble and for providing advice and guidance designed for his own best interest. As with any other guidance relationship, the inhabitant would have the privilege of switching counselors if and when there is a personality conflict or loss of mutual respect.

Life in Vacationland will be as pleasant as possible, and the standard of living will depend on the value of the work performed, the same as in the outside society. There will be wives, houses, apartments, children, movies, ball teams, swimming pools, jobs, offices, and every other aspect of a normal civilized society. The only things missing will be privacy and freedom. However the restriction of opportunity also means that it will be a lot harder to get into trouble inadvertently. There will be no fineprint in the contracts, and no easy payment plan. There will be no unemployment, and no loitering, and no crime.

People become inhabitants of Vacationland by two different ways, and they leave by the way they came in. If you are in prison serving a long sentence, you can become eligible for Vacationland after a year or two of good behavior and you can stay in Vacationland as long as you desire, as long as you obey the rules and stay out of serious trouble. However, there is one important provision, which is that the time spent in Vacationland *does not count for serving out the sentence.*

Thus a man who is in for ten years may go "on vacation" after the first year and stay on vacation for nine years. However, he cannot be released to the outside society, regardless of his behavior in Vacationland, he must first serve the remaining nine years in the penitentiary. Obviously those whose sole desire is to get back into the free society would not waste much time in Vacationland. However, others might decide that the relative advantages available in Vacationland are preferable to service in the penitentiary and freedom in the distant future, and so would choose to go on vacation.

Once a man, or woman, adjusts to life in Vacationland he is likely to remain there since return to prison becomes less attractive the older he gets. Since he is relatively happy, industrious, and self supporting in Vacationland, this represents an optimum solution for people who can't keep out of trouble in the outside society. Actually, for many people, life inside might be considerably better than life outside because on the inside they are not allowed to make serious mistakes and there are no traps to enmesh the unwary.

Freedom and security have differing subjective

values to different individuals. For some, security is much preferable. Thus, if Vacationland is properly operated, it would represent an attractive way of life for many people, despite the fact that it has a large percent of criminals in its population. In order to prevent people from committing crime just to get into Vacationland, and in order to make it possible for a man to live there in peace with his family and friends, there would be provisions for voluntary entry into Vacationland from the outside society. However, in the interests of order and security, there could be no daily movement in and out. If you want to be in, you must be willing to sign up for a definite period of time.

All violations of the rules would involve a choice of punishment, i.e., the offender can either choose to pay the penalty prescribed, or he can leave Vacationland the way he came in. However once he chooses to leave, in preference to submitting to the penalty, he forfeits his right to return. On the other hand, if he leaves "in good standing," he has the right to come back any time he so chooses.

In conclusion, it can be seen that each of these suggested approaches results in minimum cost for achieving a particular objective, and provides a maximum chance for success. Substituting solitary confinement for protracted penal service would reduce the cost of providing an effective deterrent by over 90%. Turning the job of rehabilitation over to the private agency results in a 100% savings to the taxpayer. Those that choose to live in Vacationland would provide 100% of their own support, plus payment of some State and Federal taxes on the income earned. Thus if all of these suggestions were put into operation, the only high cost operation remaining would be for those who must serve out their long sentences and are uninterested in transferring to Vacationland.

Happyland

It costs upwards to $100 a day for a heroin addict to get his fixes. Unless he is quite rich, he will end up committing criminal offenses on a daily basis, in order to obtain funds to support the habit. Considerable damage is caused in obtaining $100 each day. The damage may be physical, as with the ordinary mugging, or it may be to property, where perhaps $500 worth of goods is required to bring $100 on the black market.

To be cured, the addict must undergo a withdrawal which is extremely painful at first, but which gradually becomes bearable after several days or a week. However, the unease never vanishes completely, and a permanent cure is possible only if a more powerful mental incentive is created, and maintained which can overcome the constant temptation to enjoy the feeling of heroin "just one more time."

Society has responded to this problem in a pattern that aggravates rather than alleviates the situation. In general, the addict himself is treated with sympathy, and all of the anger is directed against the men who make huge profits by distributing the drug. Since heroin is almost as cheap as aspirin to manufacture, the men who make huge profits are able to do so only because the U.S. Government keeps eliminating the competition, thus decreasing the supply and jacking up the price.

Since this strategy doesn't work, we need a totally different approach that will work. Instead of worrying about curing the addicts and restricting the smuggling of the drug, society should merely isolate the addicts from the general society and provide them with all the drugs they desire, as long as they do enough useful work to pay for their own way. This isn't too much, since the cost of legal heroin is trivial, and the standard of living demanded by an addict is conveniently low.

If all of the addicts were removed from the open society and provided with low cost heroin, there would be no market for the smugglers. Even if they tried to create a new market by kidnapping people and forcing the habit upon them, the newly created addicts would not purchase heroin for $100 per day when they can get it free in Happyland. Thus, the existence of Happyland would stop the drug traffic completely, and addiction itself would tend to wither away as the inhabitants of Happyland grow old and die.

Happyland can be envisioned two ways. Currently fashionable concepts would see it as a super institution, a sort of combination clinic, mental hospital, and prison, where the addicts are treated as wards and continual efforts are made to cut down on the amount of heroin consumed so that the addict can be "rehabilitated" for normal society. This approach would, of course, be self defeating. Addicts would be unhappy there, and would continually rebel and escape.

A better approach would be to envision Happyland as just another city in the U.S.A., except that wages are paid partly in dollars and partly in heroin, and where no one can enter or leave without being thoroughly searched to the bare skin. In Happyland, addiction would be considered as a normal condition, the same attitude as was formerly accorded to cigarette smokers (before the disclosure of the long term health hazards).

Since the addict isn't going to be cured anyway, and since he isn't causing anyone any trouble as long as he stays in Happyland, it really doesn't make much difference if he is "cured" or not. The only valid incentives he might have for attempting withdrawal would be for personal, moral, or religious ideas, or simply because he would like to do something else with his life besides enjoying heroin. If it is his own decision, he can make it whenever he wants to and leave "cured."

It should be emphasized that Happyland should be run on a long term no profit-no loss basis. Wages would be maintained low enough so that a reasonable profit would accrue after paying all operating expenses. This profit would then be reinvested in improving the facilities and in upgrading the tools and equipment required to provide jobs for the inhabitants.

If these features are incorporated, Happyland will truly be a happy place, a place which addicts will come to voluntarily, and from which there is no great incentive to leave. Of course, there may be some addicts who enjoy the thrill of supporting their habit by acts of crime. Sooner or later these will be caught and convicted. If Happyland were in operation, a zero cost disposition of the case would be to parole them in custody of Happyland, and garnish the dollar portion of their wages until restitution of the value of the stolen goods is completed. Hopefully, they would decide to stay in Happyland, and live there a life as normal as is possible for an addict.

It is worth reemphasizing that Happyland will not be a penal institution nor a hospital. It will be a self-supporting city where the municipal authority owns or controls the means of production, the housing, and the physical access. Its charter would give the city specific authority to procure and dispense, (within the city only) unlimited quantities of narcotic drugs. Certain policies and directive authority would be exerted by the "mayor" who would be appointed by either the President of the U.S.A. or the Governor of the chartering State. Other decisions of interest only to the inhabitants of Happyland, would be handled by an internal system of representative democracy, by the inhabitants themselves.

IV

FAMILY SURVIVAL

Direct Aid for Dependent Children

A gift is a voluntary one way transfer of property. A theft is the same as a gift, except that the transfer is involuntary. Unfortunately, what is intended as a gift often ends up as a theft. This abuse occurs in individual encounters when the professional begger deceives his benefactor as to his needs. It can occur in private fund raising where those who give do not realize that most of the money goes to the fund raiser rather than to the "cause." It can also occur in public programs when the recipients include people who do not or should not qualify for the benefits. Thus the major problem with all giving, public or private, is to avoid deception and make sure that the benefit goes to the intended recipient and is used for the intended purpose.

Before the present aid for dependent children (ADC) programs were established, reluctant parents had to support their children or face prosecution under the child abuse laws. Ultimately, if the parents could not or would not take proper care of them, the children were placed in foster homes or orphan asylums. This system provided strong incentives for parents to support their children, and the overall cost to the taxpayer was comparatively low. But if a parent could not earn enough to provide the support, the penalty for both the parent and the child was quite severe.

One of the purposes of the ADC system of providing child support was to prevent the psychological damage that occurs when children are separated from their parents. Unfortunately, with the payments going to the parents, there is opportunity for parents to divert the funds to their own use. Once a parent yields to this temptation, there will be the discovery that more children mean more money, and there will be an economic motivation for increasing the number of needy children. Thus the ADC programs to alleviate poverty can actually intensify it by encouraging higher birth rates among the poor.

ADC has other disadvantages that were not forseen when it was first started. Since the benefit usually goes only to a single parent "family," there is a negative economic incentive for a two parent household. The father has to hide when the ADC inspector comes around, otherwise the family may lose their eligibility. Still another disadvantage is the adverse effect on the child's sense of right and wrong as he becomes aware of the games that his parents are playing to obtain money from the government.

The abuses associated with ADC are related to the payment mechanism. If a system could be developed that would eliminate all payments to the parent, and instead furnish the goods and services directly to the child, most of the abuses would not occur.

In other welfare programs, this principle is already being used. For instance, in some day care programs the agency will pay the day care center directly for services provided for eligible children, rather than channeling cash payments through the parent. In the food stamp program, the use of a non-cash voucher makes it more difficult for the recipient to divert food "money" for other purposes. The success of these programs shows that non-cash payment systems can be made to work.

What we need is a program for child support that would provide all of the needed services directly to the child with no payments to the parent. This could be done with an expanded voucher system which would allow the parent to procure not only food, but clothing and medical, dental, day care, and education services as needed, without handling any cash. With the elimination of cash payments to the parent, the major disadvantages of the ADC program would be eliminated, but the essential advantage of the parent-child relationship would be preserved.

One of the expected results of a program for direct services to the child would be a greater incentive for more women to enter the work force. This would mean that there will be a need for additional day care services. Some of these could be provided by business establishments that employ large numbers of working mothers. Perhaps additional day care services could be provided by the schools. If the qualification of approved day centers could be standardized and expedited, the availability of services would quickly expand to meet the effective demand provided by the voucher system for paying for these services.

In concert with an expanded day care system, there should be some consideration for keeping the schools in operation for eight hours a day instead of only six. The final two hours would be available on a voluntary basis for the children of parents who must work a full eight hour day. The extra two hours could be used for individual study and homework assignments, or for programmed activities such as remedial reading, physical education, intramural sports, etc. The main requirement is to provide properly supervised activities for the children so that they will not run "wild" on the streets while their parents are away at work. Hopefully, by the time they get out of school, they will have a parent at home waiting for them.

Thus by providing a system for non-cash voucher procurement of child support services, and with suitable expansions in the day care service system, most of the abuses of the present ADC programs could be eliminated. Properly managed, the result would be better care and service for needy children as well as a lower overall cost for the taxpayer.

Actuarial Social Security Insurance

The social security program as it has evolved in the U.S.A. is a curious mixture of enforced savings, old age and disability insurance, arbitrary benefits, and infuriating restrictions. In addition, it is a political football which is dusted off before every election in the hopes of capturing the votes of the elderly. The opportunities for real improvement are great, but our judgment of what constitutes an improvement depends on our understanding of the system and its effects upon people.

Some conservatives have claimed that the whole idea is immoral and socialistic, and that therefore the only way to improve it is to abolish it. However, the principle of requiring people to provide for their own future security is entirely consistent with the freedom philosophy. A man who spends improvidently when he is young and healthy and then when he is old and sick becomes a public charge, commits an act of fraud, since his behavior results in an unnecessary, immoral and involuntary transfer of property. Moral men voluntarily provide for their own future disabilities, but immoral men do not, hoping to use other people's funds for relief of future disabilities. Social security is a way to prevent this type of fraud, by requiring everyone to insure himself against becoming a public charge.

In this view, what is required is a true insurance program whereby everyone is forced to invest in a minimum amount of insurance, but where anyone can invest more than the minimum if he so decides. The essential role of the government is to make sure that everyone has at least the minimum protection required. The government has no valid interest in determining how much anyone's program exceeds the minimum, or by what means the insurance is provided, as long as the minimum insurance requirement is met.

This perfectly sensible objective is obscured by an overlay of politically inspired efforts to buy votes by convincing the elderly that the government will "give" them money to which they are not really entitled. The other major defect is that the desire to play God creeps into the system and the "benefits" all carry with them a long string of infuriating and senseless restrictions on personal freedom. The government usurps the right of deciding how much you can earn, at what age you must retire, and how much of your benefit you can spend for this purpose or that purpose.

Would we tolerate such arrogance from a private insurance company? Whom does the money belong to anyway?

If the payment is to be considered an insurance benefit, then the money really belongs to the beneficiary and the government has no right to withhold it. If it is a "free gift" from the government, then the government has no right to tax for such a purpose in the first place.

The obvious suggestion would be that the entire system be converted to an actuarial basis as soon as this can be accomplished. This means that every benefit must be based on the premiums paid in, and the amount of the payment itself is a contractual obligation, the same obligation that exists for the government to pay the full amount when a government bond reaches maturity. All arbitrary restrictions on what a recipient may do or not do, or for what purpose the funds are to be used, etc., should be abolished.

Premarriage Agreements

A good lawyer will insist that any contract must be complete, explicit, and understood by both parties before he recommends it to his client for signature. Not only must the contract specify the particular goods, services, or duties involved, it will also specify termination procedures to be followed for every foreseeable contingency that might affect the ability or the desire of the contracting parties to make good their promises. Putting important provisions in fine print, or concealing them by misleading phraseology, is a signal to be wary of attempted fraud. A safe rule is that if you cannot understand it, don't sign it.

The law views marriage as a legal contract. Unfortunately, most of the provisions are not made available to the contracting parties at the time they are in the process of making the agreement. If everything goes as beautifully as the love-struck couple believe, then it doesn't make too much difference that neither really knows just what legal obligations are being imposed. But if things do not go perfectly, the result can be utter disaster.

A good contract specifies all of the important considerations involved in its termination and this is done explicitly as part of the contracting agreement itself. If the marriage contract is a legal commitment, then it should not only be explicit in specifying the rights, privileges, and duties of the contracting parties, it should also explicitly specify the provisions governing the dissolution of the marriage, whether by death or by divorce.

Following this logic another step, we can see that this implies that a Will should be drawn up and signed as part of every marriage procedure, since the Will is the instrument that governs the disposition of personal and jointly owned property at the normal completion of the marriage contract. The government should require this paperwork to be in order before it issues the marriage license. By so doing, the government would protect its citizens from the endless litigation and economic losses that accompany the normal end of those marriages where the contracting parties never got around to making a Will.

However, not all marriages survive until death. Some end in divorce. Some otherwise normal marriages end in divorce simply because one of the partners goes to a professional divorce lawyer for advice. If the lawyer operates on a percentage basis, he can have a powerful motive for aggravating the situation, breaking up the marriage, and sharing the loot. This situation is not limited to the wealthy, although these provide the most extreme examples of this process. Even an average working man is likely to earn over $300,000 after the divorce takes place. If an unscrupulous lawyer can get even 10% of this, it is a nice piece of booty.

This incentive could be removed by the additional requirement that the marriage license must also include a property settlement which becomes mandatory if and when any divorce occurs. The agreement would specify the division of property, the amount of alimony, if any, for the wife (as a percentage of the husband's after tax earnings), the percentage of his after tax income that will go to the wife for the support of each child in her custody, and a formula for determining who gets which children, and what visiting rights there will be.

All of this information would be printed on the back of every marriage license with suitable blank spaces for putting down whatever the couple agree on. If they are unable to agree, they would be unable to get married!

Of course there would be nothing to prevent both parties from voluntarily agreeing to changes in the specified settlement, if both are truly willing to see a change. However, there would be no way to really force a change because the agreement would already cover every major interest in question.

Obviously, there would be little economic incentive for any lawyer to break up such a marriage, since there would be no way that he could affect the disposition of property. If he cannot affect the disposition of property, there is no basis for any incentive payment arrangement.

Thus, by a simple act of the State Legislature requiring premarriage divorce settlements to be a part of every marriage license, we could eliminate this problem which destroys the happiness of so many people.

Fraud can be minimized by spelling out *all* of the contractual contingencies. By requiring both a Will, for disposition of property following death, and a Settlement, which becomes binding in case of divorce, the government can eliminate the losses which are so characteristic of these incomplete and misunderstood, but legal, contracts.

V

EDUCATION

Minimum Achievement Standards

Most education is beneficial, but some subjects are more essential than others. Children with above normal mental capacity can afford to have the vitally useful portion of their education diluted by large quantities of irrelevant facts and busywork, which may or may not make school more interesting. However, there are just as many children with below normal capacity who cannot afford to spend the time and effort on the unimportant since they need this time and energy just to learn the vitally useful material that will have such an important effect on their future.

What is the minimum requirement to survive in our civilization? Whatever it is, this should have priority over all of the other useful but not essential material. Certainly most people would agree on the importance of some of the basics, such as the ability to read, write legibly, and be able to add, subtract, multiply and divide. Certainly minimum ethical standards as to stealing, cheating, telling lies, or assaulting other people are also essential. A knowledge of basic physics appears almost essential, at least to the point that would prevent one from electrocuting himself. How to ask questions and check the answers, how to use such resources as the library, social agencies, and knowledgeable experts might also be in the list.

It is not the purpose here to define the minimum requirement for education, it is to point out the need for such a definition. If such a list could be prepared by a recognized agency, then schools could adjust their programs so that everyone learns these basics and learns them well, regardless of how much other material they can absorb. This might prevent the graduation of high school students who still cannot read or write, add or subtract.

Equalized Education

The concept of equal education is accepted by the vast majority of the citizens of the U.S.A., and has been given legal sanction by decisions of the Supreme Court. And yet the concept remains rather undefined. What does equal education mean? Does it mean equal intellectual achievement? Does it mean identical course material regardless of interest or ability? Does education become equal when there are equal numbers of black children sitting between equal numbers of white children? What constitutes equality?

One possible definition would be that equal education exists when the same amount of money is spent in educating each child, with each child's education including a basic minimum of essential skill and information, and with the remainder of the effort being tailored to the particular needs, interests and talents of the individual student. If this were to be accepted as the definition, we would have to conclude that most children do not get an "equal" education, regardless of whether they live in the ghetto, or in the suburbs, or whether they are integrated or segregated. The amount of money spent per child varies and so does the relevance of the education to the needs of the child.

The main reason, of course, is that the public school education system provides a rather standardized product, and this product cannot be tailored to the needs and talents of each child. Also there is no way by which a parent can individually exercise any selection or control over the kind of education that is given to his child. If he wants to become involved, it must be as a member of a group, and whatever policies result from the hassle over the control of the local school board will be a collective decision as to what is best for all the children rather than an individual decision as to what is best for *my* child.

For example, the atheists fretted and fumed many years over what they considered was mythical nonsense, but what the majority of parents considered was essential moral and ethical teaching. Finally, of course, the atheists won the battle by getting the Supreme Court on their side, and now it is the religious parents turn to fume and fret at the irrelevance of the education being forced onto their children.

Majority rule or arbitrary dictums by the High Court do not change the fact that in either situation there is a basic inequality of education in that the children are not getting an education that meets their needs. The only way that education can be truly equal is for the particular needs of the child, and the particular requirements as specified by the parent, to be met on an individual rather than on a collective basis. If the government owned and operated system cannot provide this service, perhaps we should consider the proven abilities of free enterprise as a potential alternative.

If all education were done by private schools, there would be a much greater variety of education, since the supply would rise to meet the demand, as it does for every other product produced by private enterprise. This would certainly solve the problem of providing individually-tailored education programs for every taste, talent, or requirement. However this would not mean that the children were being given equal education by the State, since the rich would get much more than the average, and the poor might not be able to afford any at all.

Thus we have the situation whereby it seems perfectly possible for the State to make sure that equal dollar amounts are being spent on each child's education but where the State is inherently unable to provide the variety required, especially where conflicts exist as to what is the "right" type of education. On the other hand, we have the proven ability of private enterprise to provide an almost infinite variety of product at competitively efficient costs, but the inability to pay prevents any equalization of the education benefit.

Suppose the two systems are combined. Let the state provide an equal dollar benefit to each child in the form of a tuition credit that is sufficient to give each child a perfectly adequate education. Then let the parents select the school, public or private, that best meets the particular needs of their own children and pay for this education with the tuition credit provided by the state. If this were done, there would be true equality of education in the best sense of the words, with the state providing the funds but with the parents controlling the type of education, subject of course to state-imposed minimum standards.

Think of all of the arguments that would not take place at the school board meetings. Think of all the law suits that would not be required. Think of the riot-producing dissatisfaction with irrelevant education which would completely disappear. Everyone would be happy, getting the kind of education he feels is the best obtainable, and if anyone becomes dissatisfied, he can always transfer to a school that better meets his needs.

Thus, whether it is religion, race, talent, vocation, art, science, or whatever the reason, everyone would be free to obtain the best education possible, with an equal dollar benefit provided by the state, but with the parents determining the particular type of education that will best serve the needs of their own individual children.

VI

REGULATING COMMERCE

Automatic Feedback Control

The Constitution of the United States gives to Congress the power, "... To regulate Commerce with Foreign Nations, and among the Several States, and with the Indian Tribes." The question at hand is how should it go about this task most efficiently.

The engineers who design automatic factories, self guiding missiles, and space craft capable of unmanned exploration of distant planets have learned a great deal about the problem of how best to control and regulate, but this information doesn't always reach our representatives in Congress. This is unfortunate, because the ideas needed for sophisticated automatic control are really not hard to understand.

For instance, there are static controls, such as fences, which impede or prevent action in some particular direction. Then there are manual controls, such as faucets, which stay where you set them until you change the setting, regardless of whether the bathtub runs over or not. Then there are the automatic shut off controls, such as used in every toilet, which discharge a certain predetermined volume, shut themselves off, and then automatically recharge for the next operation.

Other types are more sophisticated. The thermostat is smart enough to turn the heat on, whenever it gets too cold, and turn it off when it gets too hot. However, it is not smart enough to adjust it to the exact right amount so that the heat stays on all of the time and the temperature stays constant. To obtain performance like that you need a proportional controller which can turn the heat up or down by an imperceptible amount every time the temperature starts to vary from the proper set point. The automatic attitude control systems in our space craft use a modification of this type of system, and they keep the space vehicle pointing exactly in the proper direction, for many months of automatic operation.

For every type of system used by the engineers to control their robots and factories, there is also a direct analog applicable for the control of commerce. For instance, a tariff is a static device much like a wall or a fence. If it is low, you don't notice it. If it is higher, it impedes travel. If it is very high, it stops traffic altogether.

As another example, the parity subsidies for the control of farm prices is like a faucet. You try to set it at the right place, but after a little while you find that the tub is running over, and you must change the setting.

Most controls imposed by Congress on commerce are based on this type of fixed level control. Regardless of where the control is set at the time the law is passed, conditions soon change so that the benefit is lessened or disappears entirely. After this happens a few times, and many dollars are spent "studying" the situation, Congress invariably sets up an "Official Board" and delegates to them the power to arbitrarily set and reset the controls as they see fit, as long as they are careful to avoid antagonizing any politically powerful groups. Thus we have the ICC, the SEC, the FAA, the FRB, and all the thousands of other alphabetical regulatory agencies. Was this what the Constitution writers meant when they gave the regulation power to the Congress of the United States? Is this freedom? Is it even Democracy?

What we really need is a little better understanding of the possibilities of automatic control. For instance, consider the control of farm prices. The basic objective is to prevent the market price from varying so wildly and so unpredictably that small farmers are ruined financially. But no matter where the price is set, it will be wrong a year or two later as market needs, production methods, and other conditions change continually. However, if the principle of automatic self regulation were applied, legislation could be passed that would properly and automatically regulate the price for years to come, meeting the desired objective without any further attention on the part of Congress.

For instance, the law could specify that every year, the average selling price must be calculated covering the previous three year period. Whenever the price of wheat falls below 90% of the current three year average price, the Department of Agriculture must buy all the wheat offered to it at that price. Whenever the price of wheat is above 95% of the three year average, the Department of Agriculture must sell all the wheat it can at that market price.

With such a system there would never be any large swings in the price of wheat, (barring a total crop failure) and all of the wheat purchased by the government would eventually find its way back on the market at a lower, or possibly a higher price. There would be no large shortages and no large surpluses. The overall cost of the price support program would be minimized. Furthermore each individual farmer would have plenty of advance warning if and when the price starts getting low and he could switch in advance to some higher paying crop.

This control principle is perfectly general, and it can be applied to all sorts of control problems, not just farm prices. For instance, the purpose of import controls is not to prevent all foreign goods from entering the country. The main objective is to prevent gross upsets in the domestic markets by sudden dumping of large quantities of imported commodities. Suppose instead of fixed quotas the law specified that the overall quantity could not exceed 150% of the average over the proceeding three years. This would prevent the dumping hazard but permit normal growth of markets where it is in the best interests of the American consumer.

The same basic principle could be used to restore gold convertibility to the Dollar, as discussed in a previous chapter. The main point here is that most control problems could be better handled by Congress itself, by way of sophisticated control legislation, rather than by delegating the function to some commission, which then becomes a little dictatorship, making its own regulations and acting as its own judge and jury. Bureaucratic commissions and freedom do not easily co-exist.

Allotment

The State and Federal governments are continually faced by problems concerning the fair allotment of scarce resources. Which broadcasting company should get the license to operate on the popular wave length? Which operator should get one of a limited number of liquor licenses? Which businesses will be allowed to pollute the atmosphere and by how much? Which taxicab company will be allowed to operate cabs on the city streets? Which transit company should be licensed to provide bus service? Which airline should get the best routes? Whose planes should be allowed to land at congested airports? Etc., etc., etc.

The socialistic way to solve these problems is to use these allotments as means to pay off political debts and earn contributions for future political campaigns. That is the way it is done. But that is not the way of freedom.

There is a general solution for all allotment problems, and that is simply to apply the principle of the free market. If the government possesses valuable resources for which there are competing interests, the simplest, the fairest, and most profitable (to the taxpayer) method is to lease them to whoever will pay the highest "rent."

Consider a fight over the valuable routes to the South Pacific. Should TWA get the route, or should it be reserved for Pan Am, or given to some other airline? Why "give" it away to anyone? Rent it! Whoever is willing to pay the highest rent gets the lease. When the lease runs out in a year or two, every airline interested gets a chance to bid for the franchise for the next two years, etc. No argument.

Which bus company gets the franchise? Let them bid for it. In this case the lease should run long enough so that the cost of buying the buses can be amortized before the bus company must face its potential replacement in open bidding for the next lease period.

Should private planes be allowed to land at congested airports? The fair answer is to require application for landing time in advance and auction off the preferred time to those willing to pay the most for the privilege.

How much should businesses be allowed to pollute the atmosphere? The same principle applies. Rent out the privilege; so many dollars for so much pollution, and keep raising the rent until the overall pollution is reduced to tolerable levels.

Every allotment problem can be solved easily and efficiently by this fundamental principle. If you really want it, you must be willing to pay more for it than the competition. Any government that gives away valuable public property at less than the fair auction market price is cheating the taxpayer as well as defrauding those who are denied their right to bid.

VII

UNLEASHED CAPITALISM

Employee Capitalism

> "But he that is an hireling, and not the shepherd, whose own the sheep are not, seeth the wolf coming, and leaveth the sheep, and fleeth;" (John 10:12)

Absentee ownership makes for an inefficient business, whether the business is herding sheep, farming the soil, or managing a large corporation. The present system of corporate ownership by millions of small stockholders makes it virtually impossible for the true owners to have any effective voice at all in the management of their company.

At a recent stockholders annual meeting, the Chairman of the Board announced that it was time to vote on some questions. Before the ballots were passed out, he felt that it was appropriate to inform the 0.1% of the stockholders who happened to be present at the meeting, that proxies had already been received representing 93.6% of the outstanding shares, all voting in favor of the management position on all of the issues in question. ". . . However, if anyone wishes a ballot . . ."

The corporation is an artificial legal person, created by special laws that grant to corporations certain rights, including limitation of legal liability, which rights are not granted to ordinary individual proprietors or partnerships. What the law has created, the law can change, and the modern corporation could stand some improvements.

What the corporation needs most of all is a healthy dose of old fashioned capitalistic ownership—management, a restoration of the normal condition where the overall strategy is to return the greatest long term profit to the owners of the business. With the growth of the super corporations, we have the condition whereby the insiders, the so-called professional managers, have total control over the corporation, and can manage it primarily for their own personal interests rather than for the interests of the stockholders.

If the corporation is large enough, and if the ownership is scattered far enough, it takes a small fortune to even mail a solicitation for a proxy to each stockholder. The managers that run the company have no difficulty in mailing out such proxy material, since they charge the expense to the company. However, anyone who has any idea of challenging their control had better have a very large supply of funds. All of which is to say, that in a large diversified corporation, there is negligible chance of a grass roots stockholders revolt. As long as the company makes some kind of profit, the insiders are as safe as a tick on a shaggy dog.

More often than not, the insiders do a much better job than is absolutely necessary to maintain their control and obtain their special "incentive" stock options. The point here is not that these men are incompetent, or even more dishonest than average. The point is that they are not accountable to anyone but themselves in any meaningful way. There is no way that the stockholders can motivate them to put the interests of the owners above that of the top management.

Of course, in many day to day operations the interests of the management is close enough to that of the owners so as to cause no real difficulty. However, whenever a crisis occurs, such as a threatened strike, a difficulty with the government, or a problem with the competition, the position taken by the management reveals whom they are really working for.

A good example of this was the great steel price crisis some years ago. The workers put it to the management for higher wages. The management explained in great detail how the cost and profit picture would not allow such an increase without a price increase, which the government would not stand for. In the end what happened? The wages were increased about 10% and the prices stayed the same. The company borrowed some three hundred million dollars to pay for additional automation equipment so that it could fire 10% of its workers and keep its labor cost the same as it was before. In other words, everybody came out all right except the stockholders who lost a good chunk of their equity to the banks and of course, the 10% of the workers who lost their jobs.

One solution to this basic problem of absentee ownership is to set up a system whereby the employees become the owners. This can be done by providing them with an irresistible motivation to invest heavily in the stock of their own employer-corporation. If the dividends earned by this investment becomes a large percentage of their total take-home income, they will cease to act primarily as "hirelings" and will start acting as owners. This means that the managers will have to justify their accomplishments, not to ignorant and apathetic stockholders who are far removed from the scene, but to men who are in a position to know all of the nitty gritties and who cannot be hoodwinked.

The machinist on the floor may not know what the president is doing, but he knows what his own boss is doing. The middle management may not be totally aware of what goes on in the shop, but they are in a position to know what goes on in the next higher level of management. Everyone is under some sort of scrutiny, and everyone has to produce.

It all sounds pretty fantastic and beyond the realm of possibility, doesn't it. How would you go about convincing every employee to invest his total savings in the stock of his own company? Is there any real way that this could be accomplished?

Since the government has created the corporation, it has the perfect right to tax corporations as it so chooses. It turns out that the government chooses to take just about half of all the profits. Then, when the stockholder gets his share of what's left, the government hits him again, this time on the basis of the personal income tax. Thus, even though the corporation might make a fat profit, by the time the stock owner gets his share, the government has raided him twice, getting 46% the first time and perhaps another 10% the second time. But who cares about rich stockholders anyway? Certainly not the average voter!

But what about the poor working man. Is it fair to tax him at a 56% rate when the expressed will of the people is that he should be taxed at a rate of 20%? Why should a poor worker, who wants to invest in his own company have to pay triple or quadruple taxes. Obviously this is not the intent of the graduated income tax!

Thus it ought to be possible to set up a system whereby the employee-shareholder would get back from the government everything in excess of the taxes he would pay if his investment earnings were taxed only once at the normal rate specified for a man of his yearly income bracket. This simply means that employee-shareowners would get back most of the corporation tax levied on their own share of the company.

If this system could be established, then the yield on a share of stock would be considerably higher to an employee-shareowner than to an ordinary investor. A stock yielding 4% to an ordinary investor might pay 10% to an employee-owner. As soon as this becomes evident, stock will be bought by employee owners, and sold by everyone else, since the other investors would need cash to be able to purchase stock in their own particular company.

After all of the increased trading dies down, we would observe the condition previously postulated, whereby every employee has a heavy investment in his own company which he cannot afford to sell. The profitability of investing in this situation is so great that men would be justified in borrowing money, even mortgaging their houses in order to take full advantage of the situation. And the more they invest, the more vested interest they would have in seeing to it that the company is successful in maximizing its long term profits.

A possible abuse might develop whereby rich investors would become token employees in order to cash in on the benefit. This could be stopped by a rule that the special rebate of the proportionate corporation income tax ceases when the income from the investment equals the wages received as an employee. This would permit investment on a massive basis by the employees, but would prevent the abuse of token employment by those who are primarily investors and not employees.

Automatic Spin-off

In the U.S.A. there is a tradition of wariness against concentration of power. When power concentrates, we get a foreboding of future trouble. Hence our anti-trust laws do not always require proof that there has actually been any measurable fixing of prices, or that there has been any actual acts directed at reducing competition, or even that there is a conspiracy to do so. All that is required is the creation of conditions of power which "might" tempt such action.

Maybe this is a good thing, but it does have some disadvantages. One of the major disadvantages is that it fosters inefficiency in large corporations, rather than encouraging them to operate at maximum efficiency.

Take the case of Du Pont. For many years they had internal policies, such as the rule of never capturing more than one-third of any chemical market, the practice of giving valuable data to competitors in order to strengthen them, and they studiously avoided monopoly situations even in products developed solely by Du Pont chemists. What was the result? The government finally decided that Du Pont's investment in GM, after 30 years of acceptability, suddenly wasn't acceptable any more! So Du Pont shareholders were forcibly divested at considerable loss in market value and tax liability. Is this due process?

It isn't that we need less anti-trust activity, we probably need more of it. The point is that the rules should be spelled out more clearly, so everyone knows what can be done and what cannot be done. It is the uncertainty which paralyzes the decision making process in industry.

Several rules could be suggested. One might be that no company can have more than one-third of the business for any market where the total sales of the market exceed .1% of the current gross national product. A similar arbitrary rule might be that no company can sell more than 1% of the gross national product. With these guidelines clearly spelled out by the law, the companies could maximize their efficiency within the bounds of the law without the eternal fear of incipient harassment.

Since everyone would know in advance when a company's growth brings it close to the size limit, there would be plenty of time to set up an orderly spin-off of a new company, complete with facilities, management, markets, suppliers and stockholders. Since the stock of the spin-off company would be initially distributed to stockholders of the parent company, it would be in the interest of the old management to do their best to give the new company a good running start, so that needless confusion and losses to the stockholders would not occur.

Needless to say, the government has an interest in promoting such spin-offs and it should make sure that there are no tax penalties. That is, the issuance of the new stock should be treated as any other stock split, with its value deducted from the value of the original stock, and with no capital gains taxes imposed until the stockholder actually sells the stock.

The knowledge that rapid growth is possible, even encouraged by the government, combined with the new opportunities for advancement associated with the formation of the new spin-off corporations, should provide considerable excitement and revitalization for some of our tired giants. It would be good for General Motors, and it would be good for the country.

The Time Bank

One of the problems that continually gnaws away at the working man is the knowledge that he is expendable, when and if business activity falls off. Thus a good bit of his union activity is directed toward protecting himself against this hazard. Hence the pressure for a guaranteed annual wage, ironclad seniority rights, and efforts to decide for management how much of the work is to be done in house and how much by outside contractors.

One of the problems that gnaw at the managers is that just when they get the big order, and the equipment is in, the workers suddenly decide to cause trouble and stop production.

The time bank could help to alleviate both of these problems. Here is how it would work. The basic idea would be to provide each worker with "surplus" vacation time, part of which would be stored up for emergencies, and part of which could be used or stored for later use at the discretion of the workers.

Let us say that a typical plan would provide one extra

week the first year, two extra weeks the second year, and three extra weeks the third year, and every year thereafter. Also, the plan would require that at least six weeks must be kept "in storage" but any excess can be stored or expended at the choice of the employee. Thus nothing unusual would happen for the first three years, while each employee is building up his "deposit in the bank."

The fourth year, each employee would find that he has three extra weeks besides his normal vacation, which he can use or store as he sees fit. If he is not very worried about his future security, he can enjoy a trip to Europe, go on an extended fishing trip, or stay at home and take out garbage for the wife, whatever he decides to do. However, if he desires security more than travel or fun, he can just leave the time in the bank and be content with his normal vacation.

The same choice occurs every year. Thus after ten years on the program, some very cautious people would have 27 weeks of full pay security stashed away in the time bank, which is theirs whenever they want it or need it. They know that regardless of the reason, they will be paid for 27 more weeks whether they work or not. Thus they are immune, at least for half a year, to any layoff, strike, secondary boycott situation, etc. They get their pay regardless.

It is a peculiar psychology, but the fact is that people are very defensive about their property and very attached to their vacation plans. Thus if and when a strike is proposed, every employee must realize that while he is on strike, the company will continue to pay him but that the time bank deposit is being used up, week by week. If he feels that there is a real important issue which must be settled, he may be willing to expend his stored security. But if the issue is not vital, in his opinion, he will vote against the strike. Why should he spend his time carrying a picket sign in September when he already has specific plans for a hunting trip in November, or a ski trip next February? Why should he use up his existing security striking for some trivial grievance?

A week of vacation is approximately equal to a 2% increase in the yearly labor cost. Thus this system would cost the company a total amount equal to an across the board 6% increase in wages. However this total would be reduced slightly by the fact that the company does not have to pay the full rate on newly hired employees. Also, the sinking fund established to provide the funds for the time bank payments, would return some interest to the company. This accumulating interest would just about match the year to year increase in the payment obligation, due to the normal increases in pay rates.

Thus if all works out as expected, the employees would get more vacation and more security, and the company could expect fewer and shorter strikes.

Strikes Against America

When a company and its employees cannot agree, the employees may strike, inflicting suffering on both the company and the employees. Depending on who hurts the most, one or both parties moderate their position and the strike is ended. However, when the strike is against an essential industry, or a vital public service, it ceases to be a tolerable family fight; it becomes a hostile act of war against the country itself. It may not always be easy to define the dividing line, but the truly general strike is the preferred weapon by which democracy is destroyed and dictatorships are established.

Since the dividing line is somewhat unclear, we observe a continual increase in collectivist action in striking against the public. First it is the transit workers, then the garbage men, then the teachers, then the police. When the army and navy get infected by this virus, we will not have to worry about being taken over by totalitarianism, it will already have occurred.

However, it is not enough to agree that strikes against vital public services should be prohibited. They already are prohibited, in many cases, yet the workers strike anyway. What's more, they generally obtain their demands, including amnesty for violating the law against striking. The basic reason is that all too often the public service employee has been left far behind in the inflationary wage spiral, and everybody including the law enforcement agency, knows it. So when they violate the law and strike, the government does not crack down and punish them, but rather compromises and negotiates trying to get the services back to normal as quickly as possible. It makes sense from a short term viewpoint, but from the overall viewpoint, it makes the laws against public service strikes completely ineffective.

Thus the first requirement for a solution to this problem is for a way to be established which will prevent the need for a public service strike. We need a system of automatic wage increases which will prevent public service employees from being left behind when everybody else is getting their wages increased.

It isn't enough to go by a fixed formula, or a cost-of-living index, or some sort of wage fixing "board." Fixed formulas cannot correctly predict the future, and cost of living indexes will not suffice to keep the public service employee pay equivalent to the pay increases achieved by other workers. A wage control board soon succumbs to charges of bias, and we are back where it all began.

Perhaps the best approach would be to monitor the average pay for equivalent work in other industries, and automatically raise (or lower) the wages of the public service employee in proportion to the changes in the moving average. This would eliminate the intensity of the pressure to strike, but there might still be wage disputes or work rule disputes which could cause strikes. For these cases there ought to be rules requiring binding arbitration so that actual strike action would not be necessary.

Finally, with the need for strikes eliminated, the government could rebuild its prohibitions against public service strikes, and make it effective by prompt punitive action against the organizers of illegal (and unnecessary) strikes. This should solve the problem insofar as government employee strikes are concerned.

However, there are many private enterprise industries whose services are essential to the health and safety of the public. How can we prevent the strike weapon from being used against the public in these cases, and still preserve the essential right to strike? This is a much more difficult problem, and any solution will be opposed by those who rely on threats to the welfare of the public as a means for obtaining more than fair or reasonable increases in their wages.

One approach might be to use the well-established principle of prohibiting monopoly. If this principle were applied to labor organizations in essential industry, it could result in rules which would prevent the simultaneous shutdown of an entire industry. The details of such an arrangement would have to be worked out by Congress, but in essence, any one labor organization, like any one business, might be limited to 33% of a particular essential industry. In addition, conspiracy for simultaneous or coordinated action by two or more unions could be prohibited the same as such activities are prohibited to other business organizations by the anti-trust laws. With such rules, a union could shut down part, but not all of an essential industry.

These prohibitions are not at all as damaging to the legitimate collective bargaining power of the unions as it might appear. If a union shuts down part of an industry, it is often a more effective motivation on management than if the entire industry were shut down. For instance, if Ford is struck, the Ford management not only is making no cars, it is also acutely aware that some of its steady customers are switching over to GM and Chrysler. If the entire industry were down, at least the management would not have to worry about loss of markets to their competitors.

Thus it is that the only significant loss of power for the unions would be the loss of their power to strike against the well-being of the public, which of course is our intent. In all actuality, the bargaining power with respect to management would not be significantly weakened.

If these actions were taken, strikes by public employees would be unnecessary as well as illegal and would therefore become quite rare. Strikes by non-public employees in essential industries might cause some shortages and inconveniences, but there would be no serious danger as would occur if an entire essential industry were shut down by a general strike. Labor could bargain with management, and labor could still strike against management. The essential difference would be that labor could no longer strike against America.

Do You Really Believe in Capitalism?

It is hard to find people who are ardent capitalists, who really have the zeal of a true believer. Every other philosophy has dedicated advocates, except capitalism. We tend to avoid this issue, and when we are pressed, we "excuse" our belief in capitalism by saying that it works out pretty well in practice, and it has raised the standard of living, and it provides an alternative to a totalitarian police state, etc. But in the end we admit that basically it is a system of organized greed and exploitation, and in a perfect society we would undoubtedly have to find a nobler, more altruistic way to get the day's work done.

Our opponents, who have a sixty year record of brutal despotism, merciless genocide and systematic torture, enslavement, and mind control, and who have never even approached the levels of efficiency and productivity enjoyed by the capitalistic countries, are somehow able to convince the nonaligned that their system is better, more moral, and in the end will triumph! Why?

It isn't simply a matter of more efficient propaganda and public relations. That is part of the answer, but it doesn't get to the heart of it. The fact is that the communists have a convincing moral argument and the capitalists do not. The result is that to the young and the idealistic, their system really sounds better than ours.

The essence of the argument is profit. Is it morally right to make a profit, or do profits represent an unfair withholding of part of the overall price which rightfully belongs to those who do the work. There is no question about the answer in the minds of communists and socialists, and to many honest but somewhat confused liberals. Profits are definitely wrong, especially large "excess" profits, and the government must take affirmative action to control or eliminate this evil tendency for man to exploit his fellow man.

If profits are really evil, then a moral idealist must go all the way and dedicate himself to the elimination of the entire profit system. This is the belief of a new convert to communism. For those who want to keep the profit system because of pragmatic reasons, the true zealot has nothing but scorn. Conversely the moderate liberal is always feeling a little guilty. He really believes that the system is wrong, but he is unwilling to embrace the alternative which he knows results in destruction of material prosperity and personal freedom.

Why are profits evil? The argument goes all the way back to the first modern economist, Adam Smith. Smith observed that the price of most goods generally stays pretty close to the cost of all of the labor that was involved in manufacturing the goods and selling them on the marketplace. This rough equivalence was later stated in a more dogmatic fashion by Karl Marx, who defined the value of any goods or service to be exactly equal to the productive labor which was used to make and distribute the goods or services in question. This seems to be an obvious truth, and people accept it with little question. Once they accept this definition, they are "hooked," and can't get free. The inescapable logic which follows this premise shows that profits really are just as Marx says—immoral, unjustifiable, and essentially evil.

Obviously if the value of a product is exactly equal to the labor cost, the capitalist who sells it for more than the cost is cheating the buyer since he is charging the buyer more than the true value of the product. On the other hand if he reduces the price to the true value, he goes out of business because he has zero profit, or he squeezes some profit out of his workers by unfairly paying them less than the true value of their labor services. The logic is plain: any profit means someone is being cheated, either the workers or the customers. The only fair thing to do is to sell at cost, and this of course means that there is no reason to be in business in the first place. Consequently the only moral system is for the government to take over and direct all production and distribution at cost, so that no profit is retained by any private individual or corporation.

The only way to combat this argument is to go all the way back to the original premise which says that the value is exactly equal to the cost of the labor required to produce the product. It is not, and it is easy to prove that it is not.

If a vacationer finds a gold nugget in a stream bed, his labor cost is practically zero, but this does not affect the market value of his nugget, which may be worth several hundred dollars. One artist may spend the same time painting a picture as another, but this does not make the pictures of equal value. One engineer may work just as hard designing a bridge as another, and yet the bridge which falls down is certainly of less value than the one which is properly designed. One doctor may spend just as much time on an operation as another, but the value of the services is not the same if the patients of one die while the patients of the other live. It ought to be quite obvious that there is no necessary relation between the labor expended and the resultant value of the product.

If the labor content does not determine the value, what does. Here again the answer is plain once we take a look at it. Value is subjective, it exists in our minds. A product has value because we desire it for some purpose. It may be beauty, which is another purely subjective concept. What is beauty? It's what we think is beautiful! And what is beautiful to one, may not be beautiful to another. Similarly with value. A product's true value depends on who is considering it, and it will be a little different to each different evaluator.

If this is true, how do we ever determine a fair price if the value is different to every different person. Of course price is not the same as value, and so the price can be agreeable to both the buyer and the seller, even though they have different ideas as to its value. In fact it is *because* they do have different ideas as to the value that it is possible for any trade to take place at all. For the seller is not going to sell if the price is less than his idea of the value, and the buyer is not going to buy unless, in his own opinion, the value is greater than the price. Obviously if they both value the object exactly the same, the price would be exactly the same as the value, and there would be no reason for the sale.

Perhaps we could use a simple example. A dime is worth ten cents. Would there be any point in selling a dime for ten cents, or trading ten cents for a dime, unless it were for some other reason of convenience. It is hard to imagine any motive for a person to go around making a business of selling dimes for ten cents, but this is what we are really saying when we say that an object should have a price equal to its true value.

Actually, of course, a dime may be much more valuable than ten pennies, especially if you must make a telephone call. We all can recognize such a situation, and it is perfectly possible that we would be glad to pay fifteen pennies for a dime if we really have an important reason to make the call.

Thus the true situation is that things have different values to different people at different times. Sales or trades only take place when the value in the mind of the buyer exceeds that which is in the mind of the seller. Obviously if the reverse were true, the buyer would never be willing to come close to the price required by the seller, and no sale would take place. However if the buyer thinks it is worth more than the seller thinks, then a sale is possible, and the price will be somewhere in between the two valuations.

Where between depends on their skill as bargainers, and on the existence of alternate sources of supply. If the seller is a skillful bargainer, he may obtain a price that is very close to the valuation that is in the mind of the buyer. However, he cannot come too close, because as he insists on a price nearly equal to the subjective value to the buyer, the incentive for the buyer to buy tends to disappear. If the seller demands a price equal to, or above the value in the mind of the buyer, then the buyer loses all interest and no sale is made. Thus we have the art of haggling.

A similar situation exists on the part of the buyer. The new car salesman may say he is very interested in making a sale, as indeed he is, but his interest fades when the buyer mentions a price that is below his costs. The salesman makes a quick decision as to whether this prospect is "serious" or not, and if he sees no chance on arriving at a reasonably profitable price, he courteously disappears.

From all of this we can conclude that most sales are made at prices that are somewhere midway between the true worth to the buyer and the true worth to the seller. Since "profit" can be considered as the difference between the price and the value, it can be fairly said that both buyer and seller make a profit. Since the seller gets a higher price than his valuation of the object, his profit is the difference between the price and his valuation. On the other hand the buyer feels that he has found a good bargain, and his happiness is proportional to his "profit," i.e., the difference between his higher valuation and the price he has to pay.

Thus the whole concept of the morality of profits depends on whether you believe in the labor theory of value or the subjective theory of value. In the labor theory, profits mean that either the worker or the customer is being cheated. In the subjective theory, every voluntary trade involves profit for both the buyer and the seller, and there is no way for anyone to know where the price should be except by a direct bargaining action between the buyer and the seller. If only Adam Smith had gone a little deeper into the subject and spelled out the subjective theory of value, what a different world this would be! For it is impossible for one who understands the subjective theory of value to ever accept the labor theory, and without the labor theory of value there could be no communism, at least not in the modern Marxist-Leninist sense of the word.

Of course the arrival at a mutually profitable trade or sale depends on the absence of force or threats of force. It is easy to see that outright use of force changes the whole process from trade to theft. Not so easy to see are the in-between stages where the use of force is less overt, and the only result is that the buyer, or the seller may be forced to trade at a price different from that which he could obtain if the transaction were purely voluntary.

In the labor theory, a fair trade requires the use of governmental coercion, since it takes a third party to "judge" what price is fair. In the subjective theory, the only unfair trades are those where a third party interjects itself, since it is only by free bargaining between the buyer and the seller that a mutually satisfactory "fair" price can be determined.

The entire motivation for each step of the production and distribution process can be traced out as a series of steps with each step resulting in an increase in the subjective value, and with each intermediate owner buying material at prices below his valuation, and selling his product at prices above his valuation, after converting the product in some way such that it will be more desirable to his potential customers. The final consumer thus pays the highest monetary price, but he also makes a profit since the true value of the product must be more to him than the price, or else he would be unwilling to buy.

Of course fraud and exploitation are possible in the subjective theory also, but only when either buyer or seller is deceived as to the nature of the product. Where such deceit occurs, the subjective value existing at the time the trade is made suffers a drastic change when the true nature of the product is discovered sometime later. Honest merchants try to avoid such situations since a cheated customer will take his business elsewhere. However, there are always the itinerant salesmen who are here today and gone tomorrow, and there are other businesses where the loss of repeat sales can be safely ignored. In these cases, fraud is not uncommon, and many deceptive practices are used to obtain "unfair" profits. In these situations the government can be of considerable service, not by trying to fix fair prices which it cannot do, but by requiring disclosure of relevant information, and by preventing monopolistic practices, agreements to fix prices, etc.

In summary, we can say that in an honest trade that is preceded by free bargaining, the price will not only be fair by definition, but both sides will necessarily benefit by the difference between the price and their own subjective valuation of the worth of the goods being traded. When there are large differences between the valuations,

TABLE I

Labor Theory of Value	Subjective Theory of Value
Value exists in the product	Value exists only in the mind of the evaluator
Value is created by productive labor	Labor is motivated by envisioned value
Value equals production labor	Value varies with the judgment of evaluators
Value is constant during distribution	Value normally increases during distribution
Value remains constant in a trade	Value always increases in a trade
Value is unaffected by scarcity	Scarcity increases value
Value is measured by labor input	Value is roughly measured by market price
Value is the same for buyer and seller	Value is always more to the buyer
Trading requires agreement on value	Requires buyer's evaluation to be above seller's
A fair price must equal the labor cost	Any mutually agreeable price is "fair"
In a fair trade, nobody profits	In a fair trade, everybody profits
A fair price equals the true value	Must be below buyer's and above seller's value
A fair price may require government action	Government interference prevents fair pricing
Buyer may pay more than the value	Buyer won't buy unless price is less than value
Seller shouldn't get more than the value	He won't sell unless price is above his value
Seller's profit equals buyer's loss	Both buyer and seller always profit
Haggling determines who gains and who loses	Haggling allocates the profit from the trade
A trade requires enforcement of a price	A trade requires agreement on a price
Seller sets price unless government intervenes	Prices are set by competition and haggling
Seller's profits imply unfair exploitation	Every trade profits both buyer and seller
Government ownership prevents exploitation	Government ownership guarantees exploitation
Profit is unnecessary and immoral	Profit is natural, moral and essential
The Labor Theory "validates" Marxist-Leninism	The Subjective Theory validates Free Enterprise

there is great motivation for trade, since the real "profit" for both the buyer and the seller can be very large indeed. Such profits, large as they may be, are entirely moral and commendable, since by definition the benefits are mutual to all concerned, see Table I.

Wouldn't it be great if this understanding were general knowledge and we wouldn't have to feel guilty about our capitalistic system of competitive enterprise? Wouldn't it be wonderful if we could start believing in the American Way again? We can, if we keep in mind the mutually beneficial characteristic of freely negotiated prices and recognize the unfair and regressive effects of third party interference. Honest profits are always mutual, and thus are entirely moral and beneficial, and this truth is what we need to uplift our spirits and create a little enthusiasm for capitalism. Competitive capitalism is a good system, not only for its material benefits, but because it is entirely consistent with morality, fair play and freedom. We have a good system—let's be proud of it!

VIII

HONEST GOVERNMENT

National Senators

Two of the best known evils of democracy are the practices of log rolling and pork barreling. "Pork barreling" refers to unjustifiable expenditures of public funds from the United States Treasury, in order to construct relatively useless roads, dams, and other building projects to pay off wealthy contractors for campaign contributions. The same procedure is applied for such projects as urban renewal, where insiders make high profits from the transfers of land, and where the poor can be put under political obligation by the low cost public housing provided. There is no end to the projects, and new ideas are invented continually. How else can the congressmen pay their campaign debts?

The writers of the Constitution worried about this possibility, but they had a system of countering motivations, of checks and balances. If any one congressman tries to get extra money for his own State or District, then the other congressmen would see through the scheme and prevent it, since the extra money for one area means that the people from the other areas are being robbed.

This all seemed logical, but it did not work out that way. The congressmen invented another little practice known as "log rolling." "You help me roll my log, and I'll help you roll yours!" In effect, each congressman is in the same boat. He has to bring "free" money back home from Washington or his opponent in the next election will win. As Teddy Kennedy said, "I can do *more* for Massachusetts!"

Of course, some congressmen are too honest to play this game of deceiving their constituents by pretending that the money is free. However, good guys often lose, and these type of congressmen rarely get re-elected. So the log rolling goes on, and the pork is distributed, lavishly if not entirely equally, and the taxpayer wonders why more taxes are needed every year to provide the same (or less) government service.

You have probably heard this same story many times before, with the rousing conclusion that, "We need better men in Congress," or "Vote the rascals out," or "The real trouble is public apathy," etc. These cliches are quite irrelevant and they do not help solve the problem. The real problem lies in our present system of congressional representation.

The basic cause of this waste is that every congressman is *forced* to put the needs, desires, and interests of his own supporting constituents above everything else, including the overall best interests of his country. Many congressmen don't like to do it, but it is a necessary part of their job. Every congressman is in the same position, each represents a section of the country. No one in congress represents the country as a whole.

This is the basic cause and it suggests an obvious cure. Why not put some people in congress who will represent the country as a whole? If there were some congressmen who were elected at large, by a system which prevented any domination by the political parties, these men would be free of the normal political debts which force the other congressmen into the scramble for pork. In effect, such men wouldn't have any logs to roll, and thus could not be punished for not supporting the waste and corruption proposed by the other congressmen.

The difficulty, of course, is that if there were only a very few of these men, they would not have the power to accomplish their purpose. If there were very many, it would become quite cumbersome to put them on the ballot, and few voters would be willing or able to pick the best hundred names out of perhaps a thousand candidates. It sounds like a good idea, but is it really practical? Is there any way to reduce the number of such representatives for the U.S.A., to a reasonable level and still have enough to be effective?

In the Senate, there is a long and controversial tradition of the filibuster. In effect, the filibuster is a veto of proposed legislation, a tactic which can slow down the passage of unwanted legislation by the determined opposition of a handful of senators.

Despite the multitude of editorials to the contrary, this is a very good thing. If one president, or five appointed judges can veto or invalidate legislation, surely it is appropriate for a minority of elected senators to have the same power.

Since the Senate is much smaller than the House, and since a minority of senators can stop bad legislation, it is obvious that the representatives for the United States should be in the Senate. If they were to constitute one third (or by present rules forty percent) of the Senate, they could exert an effective veto all by themselves. However such a large number is not really necessary, and a much smaller number of such National Senators would be enough to make a major difference in improving the situation.

Suppose we consider a number such as twenty four. Since senators are elected every two years for overlapping terms of six years, this would mean that at every election the voters would elect eight National Senators. Eight is a small enough number so that a reasonable number of candidates could be accommodated on the ballot or listed on the voting machines.

The only problem that remains is how to keep these men from becoming puppets of the party. If this happens, it would ruin the whole idea. If a political party would control their vote, they will be just as susceptible to the log rolling pressures as any other congressman. This is really the crucial part of the whole plan!

However, the cumulative vote system can be used to fence out party influence. This could be done by giving each voter eight votes, and allowing each voter to distribute his votes among the candidates as he pleases. Thus he could cast all eight for one favorite, he could split them among eight candidates, or he could give several to one, and one to several, in whatever way he decides. This would reduce the party influence to a negligible amount.

To understand how this would work is quite important. For example, consider what would happen if the Democrats listed eight candidates. Of course they couldn't list them on the ballot as Democrats; the enabling law would prohibit that as part of the effort to reduce the partisan influence. But there would be no way to stop a party from handing out their own list of preferred candidates.

But it won't work! If the Democrats list eight candidates, the Republicans could easily beat them by listing only six. Since the Republican vote would be concentrated, the final result would be that the Republicans elect six candidates while the Democrats get only two. Thus a winning strategy would require a party to list only a few candidates in order to avoid dispersal of their strength.

The motivation patterns and winning strategy are even more subtle than that. For example, the black people have about 12% of the vote, and there may be a black man running for this office. If there were only one, he would be sure to win if he had the support of the black community. However, if there were several, it might be that the votes would be scattered thinly enough so that none would win, unless they could also attract votes in the white community.

Actually there are a large number of voters who don't belong to any party. We may say that the Republicans won this election, or the Democrats won that election, but the largest part of the vote is from people who really have no firm allegiance to either party—they vote for the man they like. Thus, the winning strategy of some Republicans is to shun any reference to party at all, especially when most of the voters in an area usually vote Democratic. Likewise, a Democrat in the South may just run on his own name, so as to avoid the general hatred of the voters against the National Democratic Party.

This tactic would be valuable for winning the office of National Senator. Since every voter would know that the office was supposed to be above partisan politics, they would resent any attempt to play the game at a lower level. In fact, when you think about it, only the most outstanding public figures would have any chance at all of winning such an elective office.

In the first place you would have to be known, not in just one locality, but across the nation. You would not only have to be known, but you must also be respected for your principles and ability. You couldn't win with hoopla.

Who would these national senators be if we had this system in operation now? There is little doubt but that past presidents and vice presidents would have an excellent chance of winning such an office. We might have had Johnson, Humphrey, and Truman. Thirty million people voted for Goldwater, so there is no doubt that he could have made it. Today, Ford, Connally or Baker might win such office with considerable benefit to the country. Simon, Udall, Jackson, Kissinger and maybe even Walter Cronkite, are other possibilities.

Not only could the office of National Senator stop most of the waste and pork barreling, it would be an excellent way to make optimum use of men of high ability, dedication, and eminence, who are no longer willing or able to win a local election on the basis of spoils politics. It would also be a most excellent training ground for younger men who have the potential of becoming future presidents. The National Senator would be very similar to the President himself, in that he must be concerned with the needs of *all* of the people, and must look out for their interests in both domestic and foreign affairs.

Thus, although this change would be quite difficult to accomplish and would require another Amendment to the Constitution, it would be well worth the trouble. In fact, each of the separate benefits provided are sufficient causes in and of themselves to justify this change. We need some way to reduce corruption and stop pork barreling. We need a training ground for potential presidents. We need a place of honor and service for past presidents, and other eminent leaders. We need the office of National Senator.

Political Contributions

Corruption is the chief defect in any democracy, and our democracy in America is no exception. It takes money, lots of money, to win an important election. On the other hand, the office holder has the power to govern unfairly, if he so chooses, and he can cause some people to become richer while others become poorer. This gives the future office holder a reliable means for financing his election.

Those who contribute to campaigns where there is some sort of understanding as to the political payoff are not really giving, they are *investing.* If their man loses, they suffer a business loss. If their man wins, they make a big profit. The history of our country is filled with success stories of how men have become fabulously rich by exploiting public lands and resources with impunity, all because they made timely contributions to the right candidates.

On the other hand, those who contribute to a political

campaign with no expectation of reward lose their money regardless of whether their man wins the election or not. This situation makes it much harder to raise money for the election of an honest candidate, and makes it almost impossible for an honest man to win an election unless he is independently wealthy. Once in a while, when corruption is exposed and public indignation is aroused, an honest amateur is swept into office. But soon the public attention is diverted to other issues and the system reverts to its natural state of crooked politics as usual.

Since most politicians have to be crooked to survive, and since the public is well aware of the general situation, there is a resultant apathy at the polls. Why vote when you know that both men are equally crooked? Thus many honest folk do not often vote and this makes it even easier for the worst of the candidates to win.

When it is the system itself which favors the election of dishonest men, is it any wonder that we have such poor government? The real wonder is that we have a government with any shred of honesty at all. Fortunately most people would rather be honest, and are only as dishonest as they need to be by the press of circumstance. If it were not for this, our system of free democracy would collapse under the weight of unbearable corruption, as it has in so many parts of the world which have not had the benefits of our cultural and religious heritage.

Where the payoff is obviously shameful, the parties of the agreement go to great pains to deny the actual facts of the situation. This is the case with organized crime, graft, kickbacks, and the real estate speculation which accompanies "urban renewal." However there are situations where the payoff is considered legitimate and acceptable, and the candidate will advertise his special power or ability to benefit the voters in his constituency at the expense of the people in other parts of the country. "I can do more for Massachusetts" is a slogan which didn't pretend to seek the overall best interests of the country, but openly boasted of nepotic power, and a ready willingness to exploit others for the benefit of one particular State. But it was a successful slogan and the brother of the President won his seat on the U.S. Senate. No one protested, no one raised the charge of corruption, everyone accepted the situation as perfectly normal. Grabbing for more than your fair share is all part of the game!

Even the very meaning of the word "honesty" is changed in the politics of a democracy. Among practical politicians an "honest" man is simply one who keeps his word and pays off his supporters after the elections are over. A "dishonest" politician is one who forgets past favors when it is time for him to deliver the goods. In this esoteric meaning of the word, most successful politicians are in fact quite "honest," which accounts for their ability to attract massive financial support and continue to win elections. They are good "investments" for those who support them.

But this is not the way of liberty and justice for all. For a really honest government, the public servant must be under no private obligations, and no special interests should conflict with his sworn duty to serve all of the people equally. Thus we have the unpleasant paradox that our system for financing our elections virtually guarantees that those who win will be unfit to serve!

Of course this situation has not gone unnoticed, and there have been continued efforts to stop or limit the flow of funds from the "investing" segment of the public. If the various special interests could be prevented from making massive contributions, then the balance would shift in the direction of those who support good government with gift type contributions. So we have laws preventing large contributions by businessmen, unions, etc. But somehow these laws always seem to have some loopholes, and the flow of funds grows larger with each election. Hundreds of special "committees" pop up like mushrooms, and somehow the dollars flow to the right people, and the favors are paid on schedule. The candidate knows where the money comes from, and what he must do if he wants to survive the next election.

One of the key strategies used by the founding fathers in designing the Constitution was the principle of balanced power. If you cannot eliminate a powerful vested interest, the next best thing is to try to neutralize it by balancing it against some other existing interest of similar strength. Thus if we cannot stop the "investment" in corruptible candidates, perhaps we can find a way to reduce the importance of such "investment" by using a countervailing power. But where do we find a countervailing power that we can depend upon?

The opposite of injustice and corruption is justice and honesty, and the opposite of special interest is the general interest of the public as a whole. In other words, the countervailing power is there all right, but it is spread out over millions of private citizens. It is the public itself that is the natural enemy of special interests. Our problem is how to mobilize this dispersed power. What we really need are millions of small *gifts* from ordinary people to balance off the large *investments* from the few special interests. If gifts account for 2% of the election contributions and investments for 98%, we have corruption. But if gifts account for 50%, then there would be less chance for the crooked politicians to win.

If we could somehow persuade every voter to give $10 to the candidates of his choice, then it would be possible for honest men to compete on more even terms with those who are dishonest. If a candidate gets $10 from a million people, he has $10,000,000 with which to win a campaign, but he has no way to reward his supporters, other than by giving fair treatment to *all* of the people.

Thus the problem boils down to the question of how can we motivate many millions of people to each give a small contribution to the candidates of their choice, and prevent corporations, unions, political parties and other all-too-willing middle men from taking over the control of this new source of funds. Obviously, if an organization could control all, or part of these contributions, the benefit will be lost, and we would have made the problem worse rather than better.

An interesting example of the wrong way to do this is the recent law which provides a box on the income tax form which the taxpayer can check or not check, and which thus authorizes a diversion of money from the U.S. Treasury. The money goes into the coffers of the entrenched political parties according to a formula established by the political party in power. Not only does this scheme fail to reduce corruption, it acts to prevent the rise of any new political reform party. New parties are prevented from competing with the established parties, regardless of the degree of corruption or the disenchantment of the voters. Thus this law prevents, rather than encourages, reform.

However this shrewd scheme is well worth our study. The important thing to note is that the taxpayer can "give" without any cost to himself. If he checks the box, a dollar goes to the politicians; if he does not check the box, the dollar goes to the Treasury. It is pretty easy to make a "gift" when it doesn't cost anything, especially under a barrage of "public service" propaganda urging him to help finance the American Two Party System Which Guarantees Our Freedom.

Perhaps we could adapt this idea to the purpose of really combating political corruption. Since it isn't going to cost the taxpayer anything anyway, it is as easy to make the amount $10 as $1. However, instead of funneling the money through the Internal Revenue Service, the law should specify that the money must be sent directly by the taxpayer to the political candidates of his choice. Any contributions up to a total of $10 would be deductible, not from his income, but from his tax liability, as with the previous scheme. In other words a taxpayer who has contributed up to $10 to political candidates could take that full amount off of his actual tax payment, leaving him with the same amount of money whether he contributes or not. This full tax credit would of course be in addition to the present system of deductions and credits which provide only a partial reimbursement for political contributions.

This plan requires some amount of effort from those who wish to contribute, even though it really doesn't cost them any money. The taxpayer must go to the effort of deciding to whom he wants to send his money, he must make out a check, and he must mail a letter. It's not much effort, but it is effort. This effort serves to eliminate contributions from those who don't have a political preference and thus it tends to limit the overall cost of the program.

Not only is the cost limited, but the contributions are made only by those who are politically knowledgeable enough to have a preference. This gives added assurance that the money will go to better candidates. Thus the expected effect would be a large increase in intelligent giving for good government candidates, and this giving would help dilute the corrupting effect of those who make political investments for profit. If 10% of the taxpayers participated, this would mean that there would be about $80 million to help elect honest men to political offices.

Of course the full benefits of such a program would not appear all at once. It would take some time to attract new men into this occupation and to weed out some of the old style politicians. Crooked politicians are a hardy breed, and we probably cannot expect to ever eliminate them from the scene entirely, human nature being what it is. But it should be possible to show a real and continuing improvement.

The main hazard is that in the process of putting such a system into practice, the politicians will change the key feature just enough so that they can take over control of the funds for their own purposes. The key feature is that all contributions must be made directly by the taxpayer to the *individual* candidates of his choice, and not to *any* intermediary, such as a political party or action group. The only exception would be where there is a committee certifying that all money received goes entirely to the one particular candidate for which it is formed, "Citizens for John Doe," etc. Any compromise in this feature would destroy the whole purpose of this proposal.

Planning for Patriotism

Any system needs a certain amount of moral support to make it work. A school team needs cheerleaders as well as coaches and players. A corporation president spends much of his time trying to instill aggressive spirit and company loyalty in his managers and, if possible, into the workers themselves. Unions, churches, even revolutionary militants, all show this need by their practical emphasis on building moral, elan, loyalty, zeal, etc. The spirit gives life, and without it, any system stagnates, sickens and dies.

That fine old word, patriotism, has recently fallen into disrepute in many circles. There is nothing like indecisive leadership to discourage the troops. The futile attempt to identify a no-win Asian war with patriotism hasn't helped matters either. Instead of building support for the war, it lost support for patriotism. Patriotism is not too popular in the U.S.A. today.

And yet patriotism is not a unique aspect of an Asian war, nor is it a purely military virtue. Patriotism in its deepest sense means a spiritual identification with ones fellow citizens, a sense of solidarity, of being on the same team. In this sense, a citizen can feel "patriotic" about cleaning up the rivers or fighting organized crime, as well as about joining the U.S. Marines.

We could use a little more patriotism in America, in the sense that citizens would feel their responsibilities and opportunities to help rather than to exploit their fellow citizens. With more patriotism, there might be a greater participation in the political process, with a resultant dilution of the powers of vested special interests. We might see more personal responsibility, less littering, more casual friendliness, better cooperation between the police and the public, less toleration of racists and militants who preach hatred and bloody revolution.

Assuming this is a desirable goal, how can we bring it about? Can we do anything specific, to dramatize the importance and value and meaningfulness of being an American Citizen?

Citizenship is a very important thing, but like air and water, we take it pretty much for granted. Not so with the immigrant. For him American Citizenship is an all important goal which causes him to sacrifice home, friends, relatives, customs and culture, and endure the hardships and endless frustrations required to get himself here and qualify for naturalization. And when the day finally arrives for him to become a citizen, it is generally a very solemn and joyful occasion. From that day on, he knows that he is part of the American team!

But most of us just grow up automatically citizens by birth, and seldom have much occasion to think about it. We show our birth certificates, get out social security cards, register to vote (or not, as the case may be) and take it all for granted. We never imagine any other condition; citizenship and patriotism are words which do not really affect us very much.

In most societies and cultures there is a definite ceremony which marks the acceptance of the young adult as part of the tribe. It may be a Fraternal Initiation, a Confirmation, a Bar Mitzvah, or a primitive Manhood Test which involves courage, endurance, or an ability to stand considerable pain. But more often than not, there is something to mark the change in status—in short, there is a ceremony.

Perhaps we could use something similar to bring us together again. Ceremonies are important in our culture, from the passing out of cigars when we are born, to the various graduations, the wedding, and finally the funeral. Why not a citizenship ceremony?

Of course from a legal point of view, the legal residence, property ownership, military service and tax liability, and all of the many other privileges and responsibilities are automatic and probably should continue to be so. But some privileges of citizenship are not enjoyed by children, criminals, or the mentally incompetent, and one of these is the right to vote.

Voting membership in many organizations is distinguished from all other forms of honorary or associate membership in that voting membership represents full membership. Where the distinction is made, the voting member generally has to meet all, rather than just a portion, of the qualifications considered essential for the health and vitality of the organization. Thus the granting of the right to vote could be the point at which the natural-born citizen is finally accepted with some ceremony into a recognized full membership in our society.

If such a ceremony were established, it would take place at the time that the young adult registers.

Naturally such a ceremony would have to be completely non-partisan and non-sectarian in its form and content so that none would be offended or embarrassed. In essence, the official would ask if the candidate wants to be a full citizen of the U.S.A. with all of the attendant responsibilities and privileges, including the right to vote. The candidate would give his assent, and the official would congratulate him and give him a "Certificate of Voting Citizenship," as well as his voter's registration card. And we would have a new man on our team!

The difference between liberty and tyranny is in "the consent of the governed." By obtaining an explicit consent that the young adult is willing to assume full citizenship, with its attendant privileges and responsibilities, the new "citizen" becomes part of the team as a voluntary contractual action on his own part. This does not automatically guarantee that he will in fact live up to his responsibilities for being a good citizen. But it will help. It is the fine distinction between a volunteer and a conscript, a free "citizen" or a passive "subject." And it does make a difference.

IX

WHAT CAN WE DO ABOUT COMMUNISM?

Planning for Victory

No one who spends even a modest amount of time studying the nature of communism in detail can believe that there is any reasonable hope of moderation of its dynamic thrust for domination. Communism is an idea, not a nationality. Communism is our enemy, not the Russians, the Chinese, the Czechoslovaks, or the people of North Viet Nam. Individual communists die, but communism lives on, stronger than ever.

Few people in the U.S.A. spend much time studying the nature of communism. It does not produce happiness to become aware of cruelty, hatred, terror, and hopelessness. These are living realities for a thousand million people.

We want to think happy thoughts. If we must think of horrors, we prefer to think of horrors safely past such as Hitler's slaughter of the Jews, but not current horrors such as the genocide of the Cambodian people, or future horrors such as the liquidation of our own selves and the brainwashing of our children when the communists finally take charge of our country.

The time is long past when we could solve this problem the way we solved the problem of Hitler. There will be no well matched open military struggle between communism and what was once called the Free World. The struggle will continue to be primarily by propaganda, humiliation, degradation, infiltration, and internal betrayal. Military action will occur, but only after defenses have been neutralized by political détente or by sophisticated "unilateral disarmament," that sabotage which spikes our guns without our awareness of what is happening.

We are like those who have been smoking cigarettes for 25 years, and have successfully laughed off the worry warts who were always telling us how dangerous it was. Except today, we cough up a little blood. Do we still have a chance? Our chances are not very good.

And yet the way to win exists. The winning strategy can be developed, and an approach to such a strategy is outlined here. But the prognosis is poor because our minds are numb with problems and alarms, and we, as a nation, keep ourselves unaware by means of tranquilizers, alcohol, and TV laugh-ins. We lose simply because we, as a people, cannot keep our minds on this unpleasant problem.

But whatever may be said about people as a group will not necessarily be true for people as sub-groups, or people as individuals. Thus our only hope is that those few people who *can* understand will recognize their responsibility, and not depend on others. The U.S.A. has the largest number of enlightened anti-communists in the world, even though they may only be a small fraction of the total U.S.A. population. Therefore, the essential requirement is that we shake off our habits of depending on the mass media to make our decisions, and start convincing the media to accept our proposals for victory.

Each of us should go to the trouble of compiling his own list of what he thinks should be done to win against communism. These lists should be compared, discussed, argued, and finally some areas of general agreement hammered out. My list is shown on Table II. When will you have yours?

If every citizen who is concerned about communism would make such a list, and keep revising it as his understanding is daily enlarged, then it will be comparatively easy for each of us to recognize each other and also recognize those whose actions are hurting our cause. If we cannot even define our own opinions, we will inevitably have them defined for us by those few activists in the mass media, and in Congress, whose every word and every action is consistent with the Communist Party line.

TABLE II
A PLAN FOR VICTORY

A. Short Term Goals

1. Weed out communists who have infiltrated our government.
2. Investigate political bribery by Soviet and Chinese agents.
3. Deny or impede physical access of communists to the U.S.A.
4. Eliminate all aid to communist countries.
5. Reduce or eliminate trade with communist countries; at least make them pay cash.
6. Investigate and confiscate all ownership by communists of strategic businesses, and especially communications and mass media in the U.S.A.
7. Eliminate all propaganda material coming from communist countries, and deny the use of the U.S. Mail for such purposes.
8. Provide a mandatory CIA escort service for all travel by communist nationals in the U.S.A.
9. Give generous military aid to nations willing to be publicly anti-communist, and especially to those menaced by communist armed forces.
10. Deny all military aid to neutralist countries.
11. Recruit foreign nationals who are anti-communist as volunteers in our armed forces.

12. Support the military efforts of guerrillas who are trying to regain control of their native lands from communist overlords.

B. Medium Range Goals

1. Demonstrate freedom based solutions for social problems.
2. Reverse trend toward collectivism in the U.S.A.
3. Establish a tuition credit system to give free enterprise a fair chance in elementary education.

C. Long Range Goals

1. Mount and sustain a persistent and sophisticated ideological attack against the theoretical basis of communism, to destroy the faith of the communist theoreticians, and to cause them to defect to our side.
2. Maintain an internal attack on a slightly less theoretical basis designed to keep the college level intellectuals on our side.
3. Develop and establish better anti-communist action organizations with due regard for feedback, credibility, and public relations.
4. Develop and refine the two level government system, where the States, rather than the Federal Government, would have precedence in local matters of custom, mores, culture, and "rights" not specifically included in the Constitution, and where the Federal Government would concentrate on non-sociological affairs.
5. Exploit the ability of our two level system of government to integrate the political and economic affairs of differing peoples, while maintaining and guaranteeing their rights to determine their local customs, by expanding the U.S.A. by means of mutually agreeable political union with other friendly countries.
6. Never ending prayer to God, to save us from the results of our own folly and from the purposes of organized evil.

Communists in the Government

The tragic thing about the Joe McCarthy episode, which many have overlooked, was the effect it had on our country. The public reaction to the whole problem was expertly manipulated with complete success by those whose interest was not in making anti-communist investigations more responsible, but in eliminating them altogether.

The executive order by President Eisenhower requires administration employees *not* to testify before Congress on the question of communist infiltration, without approval from higher echelons in the Administration. This has protected existing communist cells, and facilitated the proliferation of other cells within the government.

The Otto Otepka case is well known, and all of the horrible details will not be repeated here. His "crime" consisted of ignoring the gag order, and giving Congress the suppressed information regarding the hiring of certain well known security risks for high office in the State Department. His "punishment" included a complete stripping of all duties and authority, destruction of his security team, and persistent vilification in the liberal press.

The first priority should be given to amending this executive order, providing a reasonable modification which would permit Congress to get the facts but would also protect innocent people, including liberals, from the McCarthy type of harassment. The easiest way to insure this would be to modify the executive order such that testimony before Congress would be required only when the hearings were closed to the TV media. This would shut off the TV attention, but still permit Congress to get the information.

Communist Citizenship

Citizenship implies allegiance to a certain country. People renounce their citizenship when they become citizens of a hostile state; there is a definite transfer of allegiance. Such voluntary repudiation of U.S. citizenship is not common since U.S. citizenship is considered a valuable thing to have, even by those who are trying to destroy us.

The essential difference between a leftist liberal and a true communist is that the liberal wants to "improve" the form of government in accordance with his own ideas, while the communist wants to overthrow and destroy the government and replace it with an authoritarian dictatorship. The liberal can honestly swear allegiance to the flag and to the country, but the communist cannot. Thus anyone who voluntarily chooses to become a card carrying communist has in reality renounced his allegiance, and with it his moral right to U.S. citizenship.

Congress should recognize this reality by suitable legislation which revokes the citizenship of avowed communists after a certain date, giving them a reasonable time to make up their mind to either quit the Party or suffer the consequences. Those who quit, could certify that fact to the government and prevent the loss of their citizenship. Those who refuse to quit, would automatically lose their citizenship after the grace period, and would then be required to register as enemy aliens under existing registration laws. Anyone who joined a communist party in the future would do so knowing that the act includes the renouncing of their U.S. citizenship.

Assuming that this legislation was passed and tested out in a competent court for constitutionality, it would provide our government with a much needed power for dealing with open sedition. In case of a military emergency, it would provide the government with the power to apprehend all known communists as a precautionary method of preventing widespread sabotage of electric power installations, transportation, water supplies, etc.

U.S. citizenship and communist party membership are inherently incompatible. Recognizing this by appropriate legislation might not eliminate all of our communists, since there would be evasions, false statements, etc. But it would clarify the issue, it would give our security people the right to prosecute known leaders who violate the law, and it would greatly constrict the power and activity of the communists in the U.S.A.

Access

Physical access to the United States is perhaps the single most important factor in the success of communism and in our gradually accelerating subjection. Because we give them open access, they can budget billions of dollars for their business agents to purchase key control of certain essential private enterprises. When they achieve control of several businesses, they can use the finances of those businesses to aid in extending their influence and control to other businesses. There is no area, except perhaps in some parts of the armed forces, where this process of purchasing control cannot be made successful, if it is done on a gradual basis.

Have you ever considered what would prevent a determined well financed effort from achieving influence in the faculty of any typical university? We know that the communists made strenuous efforts to take over our labor unions, achieving only a partial success because of the strenuous efforts of loyal labor leaders who saw the danger just in time.

Suppose a seminary established for the training of ministers of the Gospel were to find itself under implicit obligations because of heavy contributions from a dedicated supporter. Couldn't that supporter have some influence in appointing members of the ruling board? How many ministers have you heard coming right out in open opposition to the thrust of world communism, compared to those who slavishly follow the party line?

Suppose the well funded Russian agents, acting through their stock brokers, bought up controlling interest in CBS, NBC, and ABC. Suppose they used their voting rights in these enterprises to put in directors and managers whom they knew would slant the news in their direction. Would the people perceive the distortion as the result of a planned subversion, or would they dismiss such ideas as "paranoia" and either ignore the bias or attribute it to other causes?

Nearly all of the "news" in our newspapers comes from just two wire services. If you had a budget of $10 billion a year, do you think that you could have your agents purchase working control of those two enterprises?

How much money does it take to elect a senator from a sparsely populated state? If you had an unlimited budget, could you not influence the "peoples choice," especially where there are not many people to finance the opposition? How is it that such conservative, even reactionary regions of the country, produce such devotees to the party line?

The beauty of this approach is that the man you select does not have to *be* a communist, he just has to happen to *agree* with the immediate objectives which serve the long range interests of communism. If he does that, then it is better if he isn't carrying a card; he can put on a much better performance of righteous indignation when his loyalty is questioned.

Access also enables communist police to operate in our country. Each year thousands of people quietly disappear in the U.S.A. Sometimes the news will carry a story in which some refugee or other is rescued when the police detect Soviet agents in the very act of kidnapping. How many are not detected? How many people want to defect to the "safety" of the U.S.A. but don't because it means that they must stay in hiding for the rest of their lives.

Have you ever heard of a Soviet agent being convicted and punished for attempted kidnapping?

In addition to being able to legally own and control American businesses, and being able to enforce their "law" in selected instances within the U.S.A., the communists are saving billions of dollars in technological research simply by picking up ordinary information which is free to anyone in our open society. Technological journals, reports, patents, new models of equipment, detailed disclosures in bids, every non-classified piece of information is there for the having. They simply bundle up the stuff and take it home. This saves their engineers for the key war industries, where they are forging ahead and must develop their own information since they already know all of ours.

This is not to say that they do not also get the results of our classified research; it is just a little more troublesome. They got the atom bomb information before we even knew the bomb would work. Their penetration of our security is so universal that any document with a wide distribution is considered compromised after a period of a few months.

The problem is not to eliminate such penetration; total elimination is theoretically impossible. The problem is to reduce the *amount* they get. This problem comes right down to the question of access. If we deny access, they get a lot less information. We should keep their agents out of our country!

Aid and Trade

Aid and trade with communist nations should be reduced or stopped altogether for the simple reason that this will hurt them more than it will hurt us. Why should we dig the grave for them to bury us?

It is impossible to make an argument against aid, or trade, without encountering the "Moderating Communism" myth. This myth projects a vision of the future, where all nations live together in peaceful coexistence. Every squabble within the communist camp, every evidence of consumer production increase, every peace offensive is hailed as proof that finally, progress is being made. And every such campaign falls on its face, as the bloody power of communism stomps out even the beginnings of freedom in East Germany, in Hungary, in Czechoslovakia. How often can people swallow the same stupid lie?

The reality is that the communist ideology has an automatic internal feedback mechanism which wipes out what they call "revisionism" whenever it becomes a potential problem. The techniques of "hard" communism are stronger than the survival capabilities of "soft" or revisionist communism. The dynamics of power insure the condition where the "bad guys win." Thus, whenever any internal deviation toward softer policies develop, there is an automatic and inevitable internal power struggle which yanks them back to the original purpose of totalitarianism and conquest.

Total collapse, violent revolution and chaos in a communist country is more probable than moderation. This is because the inevitable result of giving slaves a little freedom is that they want more faster, and soon they want all, and now! Thus if the revisionists ever survive the threat from the hard liners, the entire structure would be abolished by a true people revolution which would wipe out all of the communists, hard, soft, or medium, as happened in Indonesia. The lives of the communist's leaders are at stake, and most of them are smart enough to realize it.

Freedom Works

Freedom works, and it works extremely well. But it doesn't solve every problem all by itself. The main mistake made in the past by those who love freedom resulted from the fact that they could usually see the possible damaging results to freedom from the solutions to social problems generated by the socialists. They saw these hazards more clearly than they could see the problems themselves. In almost no case could they see any alternative solution which might have alleviated the problem and still preserved the essential reliance on freedom principles.

This gave the socialists their winning ploy. Pick a problem. Publicize the problem. Publicize the socialistic solution. Get the reactionary backlash. Sell your program, not on the basis that it will work, but on the basis that you are concerned about people, and your opposition is not. This ploy has worked over and over again, and it still works, just as well as ever.

Those who love freedom, love it because it does solve people's problems, far better than any other general solution. But we have to become concerned with the edges, the gaps, the areas of injustice and inefficiency, where pure laissez faire just doesn't do the job. There is an essential place for government: freedom itself cannot exist without government, and a strong government at that. The main, if not sole, justification for government is to defend freedom and establish justice, and it is our business to see to it that it does the job it is supposed to do.

If we can find effective solutions to the problems of unemployment, inflation, crime, welfare, pollution, and broken homes, that work with the principles of freedom rather than against them, we will start believing that our way can, should, and will be "the wave of the future," the "historical necessity," etc. It is not enough just to believe. Faith without works is dead. We have to show practical, freedom-oriented solutions for every problem of general concern.

If freedom-oriented social solutions can be generated, sooner or later someone in power will make use of them. If and when this becomes a habit, then the trend toward collectivism in this country will be stopped. Once we ourselves have our own ideology in good working order, we can start selling it to the rest of the world. But as long as the principles of freedom remain identified with a lack of concern, rightly or wrongly, we have lost the battle.

Free Elementary Education

It is the early years where mental patterns are set which last a lifetime. It is no surprise that the product of a government owned and operated school system should believe that government ownership and operation of businesses and services is the natural, moral way to organize things.

When the communists take over a country, as they did in Cuba, the first thing they do is to go after the youth. Thousands were shipped to Russia for brainwashing and indoctrination in communist ideology. The Roman Catholic Church was able to withstand the tidal wave of Protestant Theology, but not without isolating, protecting, and indoctrinating its own children in its own schools.

What good does it do to write letters to editors, to maintain journals for the study of freedom, to debate, and to spread the word. For every convert you make for freedom, the public school system is graduating a thousand young people who are thoroughly indoctrinated in the latest liberal interpretation of environmentalism, moral relativism, humanist theology, and situation ethics; all aspects of Marxist-Leninism.

If equal education benefits for every student were insisted upon, by way of a tuition certificate or tax credit program, then non-public school students would receive the same dollar benefit for education as would public school students. Everyone would then be free of economic coercion in choosing their school. Undoubtedly many would continue to use the public school, believing that it best meets their needs. But many would shop around and some would find private schools which meet their own needs better. Freedom of choice is what it is all about, and when you remove the economic coercion you can then have full freedom in education.

In passing, it should be emphasized that this is not just a religious need. Black people would like to be in control of their own schools, and a tuition certificate plan would give them that right. Special remedial schools, or special talent schools would improve the overall relevance of the education offered. But the greatest thing from the point of view of freedom is that everyone would not be stamped by the same mold, everyone would not be indoctrinated to the same pattern of myths. It would no longer be possible to find "truth" by identifying the applicable liberal cliché. Truth would have to be hammered out as islands of agreement in a sea of healthy controversy.

The Ideological Offensive

In the dynamic phases of a communist takeover it is not uncommon for the masses of the people to be forced to spend several hours each week, sometimes several times a week, listening to endless lectures on Marxist-Leninism. To us, this seems a pointless waste of time. But they know that it is not pointless, it is essential. You cannot get creative, enthusiastic, self-sacrificing loyalty without faith. And "faith cometh by hearing."

Since we are fighting this faith, this communist religion, we must carry our ultimate assault against the heart of this faith. We must out-argue the communist theoretician on his home grounds, refute his position, and hammer home the refutation, over and over. If, as we believe, he really is wrong, then we should be able to prove it to him. If we don't have that capability now, then we better develop it, or give up the whole struggle.

Assuming that the capability can be developed, it must be practiced and refined until we have a message which reaches the very soul of the theoreticians and the intellectuals. It may be quite a different argument than the one which we would find convincing for ourselves. However, the essential requirement is that it must break the faith and destroy the ideological confidence of the communists.

Since such a message can only be developed by trial and refinement, there is no way of knowing the content of the final product. But there is a place to start, and that is at the central core of Marxist ideology, their so-called "Labor Theory of Value." This subject was previously discussed in the section entitled "Do You Really Believe in Capitalism." We know that the Labor Theory is totally inadequate to explain the real world, and we also have the Subjective Theory of Value which is consistent with reality. As noted before, it is virtually impossible for anyone who is familiar with both ideas to maintain any real belief in the Labor Theory. But the Labor Theory is essential to communist ideology. Thus a lack of real belief in the Labor Theory means a concurrent lack of real belief in communism.

The way to win is to subvert the enemy! Let's tell him about the Subjective Theory of Value. Let's tell him over and over again. It should be on every Voice of America broadcast. It should be on Radio Free Europe. It should be on every media that crosses over the Iron Curtain.

It doesn't really matter if they don't want to listen. This idea is so simple that it can be made the subject of a good old American high pressure advertising campaign. We can beat it into their heads whether they like it or not! Once they really understand, they cease to be real communists and become "token" communists. When enough of them have lost their faith, they will overthrow their slave masters and set up a more reasonable system of government. This is the way by which we can have victory without firing a shot.

Anti-Communist Organizations

Any anti-communist organization which becomes the least bit effective will be the target of a well financed smear campaign. If it were otherwise, then there would be no real internal communist menace. This fact provides a great temptation for the leaders of anti-communist organizations to shrug off honest criticism and it makes them insensitive to the feedback of information so vitally required for effective action. It surrounds the organization leadership with "yes men," and the end result can be a series of wild goose chases after unimportant, or even self defeating objectives.

Ultimately a prerequisite objective for any anti-communist organization is to obtain good public relations and credibility. If the public is unready to believe a certain truth, then insistence on shoving it down their throats is self defeating, especially if the "truth" involves a subjective evaluation of other men's motives. We should not imply that other people are communists, or traitors, unless the proof is enough to convince the majority. Most of the deeds which help communism are done in all sincerity by non-communists who have no malicious intent. Charging them with evil motives doesn't help at all.

If anti-communist organizations already existing and new ones being formed can only profit from previous mistakes, it may be possible to organize the considerable resources available into a force that can delay or reverse the communist program for the enslavement of the world.

Free World Government

Other sections in this book describe the exciting long range goal of a truly free government which might include most (but not necessarily all) of the free nations of the world in a mutually beneficial and voluntary political unification. This is presented as a fourth alternative in place of a communist conquest, or the eternal wars of competing nations, or the hopeless task of converting an association of independent nations into a political unit by endless negotiations, intrigue, and civil war. Our opportunity lies in the concept of the separate spheres of responsibility which properly exist between our States, and the Federal Government. This makes an ideal framework for an expanding commonwealth of freedom.

A nation bent on expansion by conquest can afford to ride roughshod over the local customs and destroy the local culture. However, a nation cannot expand peacefully if the new citizens have to make themselves over into the image of big brother. Thus, a prerequisite for a voluntary union is the firm conviction that such a union will not interfere with local rights, customs and culture.

We have been gradually abandoning this concept of separate responsibility for State and Federal governments. In doing so we are destroying the local freedom of our own citizens to govern themselves. Even worse, we are destroying the hope of a future where true law and justice could be provided by a free, multinational United States of the World. We should reverse this trend!

Help from God

Our concepts of freedom came from people who believed that they knew God and were loved by God. Without God, the whole idea of freedom shifts out of focus and becomes a vague expression for having one's own way. Right fades, and might takes over, and we have lost the battle.

If freedom is of God, and if God cares about freedom, then it is reasonable to expect that He will listen when we pray for it. Of course many people cannot pray because they do not believe. But of the people who are concerned about freedom, there are many who also believe in God. Sometimes this belief is a living reality, sometimes it is a little vague. So many people are told that God is dead, in their own churches, that it is no wonder that they are confused.

If we are to pray effectively for freedom, we ought to be a little less confused about our own theology. One way to do this is to get out your own Bible and study it for yourself instead of depending on others to do it for you. By understanding what your Bible says to you, you will not be so confused by what other people try to tell you.

Prayer does change things. The Bible assures us that if we ask for help and guidance, we will surely receive it. We need to ask.

X

THE UNITED STATES OF THE WORLD

Sophisticated Organization

The ability that commands the highest reward in any society is the ability to create management systems for coping with otherwise insurmountable problems and complexities. The greatest advance, and the most sophisticated organization ever developed was the two level Federal-State dual government system invented by the Americans in 1787.

The proper purpose of government is to establish law, order, justice, and freedom. Few governments are able to do all of these things well. In Russia there is more order and less crime than in the U.S.A., but there is also less justice and freedom. In our "Wild West," there was considerable freedom, perhaps license is a more accurate word, but there was little law, order, justice or security.

Whenever one government is outstandingly successful in establishing optimum conditions, the general welfare of its inhabitants rises so fast that people in other countries are consumed with desire to participate. This desire overcomes their natural love of their own country, relatives, and friends and everything is abandoned just for the privilege of immigrating to the land of promise.

The people vote with their feet for outstandingly successful government.

When the land of opportunity is empty, such immigration is acceptable, even desirable. But when the land is full of people, the new immigrants often find themselves penned into a corner of a ghetto, and never realize the happiness they expected. Far better for them, if they could have stayed home and gained the advantages they seek by a political union of their homeland with a government system that can provide the conditions of excellence.

It should be obvious that the only government that deserves to expand geographically is one that can better satisfy the needs of *all* of the people in the expanded territory. This principle is often given lip service, when the real purpose of expansion is to gain more slaves for the elite to exploit. This holds true whether the elite is the Nazi Party, the Communist Party, or the Bank of England. The true purpose is quickly evident, however, by the treatment given to the new citizens. Are they treated as full equals, or are they given a second class status?

There may be some truth in the argument that an underdeveloped area will benefit economically by becoming a colony of an enlightened and tolerant empire. But the galling abrasion of integrity, dignity, and personal freedom produces violent resentment and all of the material benefits seem of little value as the natives prepare to revolt. The revolt itself often means a drastic drop in living standards, but when has a former colony ever applied for reestablishment of its former condition after the revolt? They continue to prefer poverty, rather than a prosperous union with second class citizenship.

First class citizen status is what it is all about, not just political independence. If the empire could find a way to give this equality of status, then the main motivation for separation would be gone. The Romans understood this and they granted the right of equal citizenship to great numbers of people in conquered lands, after first assuring themselves of their fidelity and loyalty, etc. If the English had quickly given the American colonists proportional representation in Parliament, who knows what the world would have been like today!

However, an empire where everyone truly has equal rights and opportunity is really a commonwealth, not an empire at all. Consider, for example, the status of the natives of a formerly independent nation which was annexed by the U.S.A. If a school teacher in the formerly free and independent Republic of Texas can become our President, there can be no implication of second class citizenship here.

However there is one other thing besides first class citizenship, and that is survival of local culture, custom, and mores. If the people of the greater commonwealth do not have considerable tolerance in what they consider acceptable they will almost certainly try to use the power of the Federal Government to bring about conformity with their own ideas of what is right, regardless of the ideas of the dissident locals.

Suppose the United States should expand and unite with Mexico, Canada, and all of Central and South America. Would we tolerate bull fights? Would we prohibit female visitors to prisoners in Mexican jails? Would we prohibit laetrile? Would we also try to integrate the white people on the plateau of Costa Rica with the black people who live on the coastal region? How would our bureaucracy enforce a racial quota system for workers building roads in Brazil, where people aren't quite clear whether they are mostly negro, or white, or indian, or mixed?

The original constitutional division between the Federal Government and the State Government was crystal clear. In the words of the Constitution itself, "The powers not delegated to the United States by the Constitution, nor prohibited by it to the States, are reserved to the States respectively, or to the people." These words have never been removed from the Constitution, they have just been ignored. The judges of our Supreme Court place themselves above the Constitution as the supreme law of the land, in direct violation of Article VI. Why should they bother with the Tenth Amendment?

If we could ever get back to the so-called "narrow interpretation," just obeying what the words in the Constitution clearly state, we would have a much more tolerant and adaptable system of government. Assuming that adequate safeguards could be established against a repetition of judicial usurpation, the two level Federal-State system could then be successfully applied to accommodate the widely varying customs that will confront any free world government.

World government is advocated by those who see it as the only way to prevent a world war. World government is opposed by those who see it as a prime threat to their culture, their self government, and their freedom. If a model could be developed that would demonstrate success in preserving freedom, culture, and local self government, and still provide the security and opportunity of an expanded and cooperative commonwealth, such a model would satisfy all, rather than just a portion of the requirements for a truly free world government.

The Affiliated Nations Program

The people of the United States have three reasons for an intense interest in the underdeveloped nations of the world. We are interested in mutual trade because mutual trade brings mutual benefits. We are also interested in their progress for purely altruistic reasons. Our third reason is that their weakness invites communist penetration and takeover, and this constitutes a threat to our liberties as well as theirs.

All of these reasons are important, even compelling.

They have convinced the American taxpayer that it is in his best interest to invest billions of dollars in aid. The objective of this aid is to strengthen these countries to the point where they can take off on the upward curve of rapid technological progress and improving living standards.

Unfortunately things do not seem to work out the way they were forecast, and most of the progress is lost in the turbulence of population explosions, political upheavals, flight of capital, expropriations, and other troubles. Often too much is spent for prestige items, show places of heavy industry, military power, etc.

Our mistake is to think that government and technological progress have no necessary casual relation. This mistake arises from lack of understanding of the absolute necessity for governments that can provide stability, law, order, justice, and freedom.

It doesn't matter how much money is poured into a country if the government is inadequate. The money will quickly go into the pockets of the insiders, and just as quickly leave the country for investment where the risk is less and the returns greater. It is perhaps more unreasonable for a native to invest in his own country, where he is able to assess the high risks, than it is for a foreign investor, who suspects the risks are high but has no first hand information of how high.

Thus the characteristic result of political instability is that investment risks are high. Where risks are high they prevent most ordinary, long term, reasonable return types of investment. The only money available is for a fast buck, where the situation promises to double your investment in six months or a year. The fast buck gamblers who will invest in such situations will also pull out on a moment's notice, or even worse, use mobster type violence to protect their investment and maximize the gain. This is not the type of capital that is needed in the underdeveloped countries!

The cry of these countries is for honest investors who will be satisfied with a reasonable but not exploitive rate of return. Their ideas of what is reasonable are naturally based on rates of return commonly observed in the more developed nations of the world. What they do not see, and don't want to see, is that these lower returns are based on lower risks, due to the existence of well established stable governments.

Obviously, the place to start is not with the problem of getting capital, it is with getting reliable and reasonably efficient government. But this depends on all sorts of long range prerequisites such as a tradition of law observance, a tradition of peaceful elections, extensive education, opportunity for all citizens, and a patriotic commitment to the country and to the governing establishment. But all of these things are nearly impossible to establish without a reasonably adequate and stable government. Thus we have a vicious circle; progress requires good government, but good government comes only after considerable progress has already occurred.

If it were possible to work out a temporary union, whereby the underdeveloped country becomes an integral part of the United States for a specific period of time, such a period could provide just the essentials needed to break this vicious circle. The knowledge that the union was temporary would give the required assurance, similar to the money back guarantee that is so essential in the mail order business. The specification of a particular period of time would also give interested investors enough advance knowledge so that they could invest with perfect safety, knowing that they will have plenty of advance warning to recover their investment before there is a return to a higher risk situation after the temporary union is over.

Some industries normally recover their investment and start to clear pure profit in five or six years. Some require longer periods of time. The type of investment that would be attracted by a twenty year period of guaranteed stability would not come in if the period was only five or ten years. However, most businesses would be sufficiently enticed by a twenty year guarantee, as much perhaps as by a thirty or forty year guarantee. So twenty years might be a good compromise for a trial union.

During the twenty years of union, the Affiliated Nation would have all of the rights and privileges of an ordinary State in the Union, plus whatever special rights, exemptions, privileges, etc. that were negotiated as part of the treaty. Thus, unless specifically exempted by such provisions, the new citizens would vote for their local government, and also for their proper representation in the Federal Government. They would pay the same taxes, be subject to the same military service, and have all of the duties and the rights, the same as any other American citizen. They would, in fact as well as in theory, be citizens of the United States as well as of their own Nation, for the duration of the treaty of affiliation.

Some areas of difficulty immediately arise. One is the possibility that swarms of ordinary citizens from the U.S.A. would move into the newly affiliated territory, buy out the local inhabitants, and take over the country as we did with the Indians, and as the Zionists did with the Arabs. Another is that the inhabitants of the newly affiliated nation might decide to mass emigrate to get in on the very liberal unemployment and welfare programs provided by our more improvident cities. Needless to say, both situations are undesirable but perfectly possible.

This hazard of mass emigration and immigration could probably be handled by a clause in the affiliation treaty which would establish restrictions of such movements, and give each of the two parties the unilateral right to restrict, control, or establish eligibility requirements for immigrants who wish to settle permanently and establish local citizenship and residence. Thus the Affiliated Nation could take this action by its own local government. The U.S.A. could also establish additional restrictions, if it so chose, and in the voting on this issue, the representatives from the Affiliated Nation would naturally be excused.

The other major area of difficulty which can be visualized is what happens when the treaty nears its termination. There will be literally billions of dollars of investment, and there will be those who view the coming re-establishment of the "right of expropriation" with greedy anticipation. The investors will also foresee the day of expropriation and will naturally try to reduce their losses by cutting back on modernization and maintenance and concentrate on just keeping production going until the treaty terminates. By this strategy, so analogous to the motivation pattern of the ghetto property owner, they would hope to minimize the final losses when the property is expropriated.

Thus, when the treaty terminates the investors stand to lose, but not very much, and the expropriators stand to gain, but not as much as they would like. In any case, the last ten years of the treaty will not be as happy or as beneficial as the first ten years.

It might occur to everyone, after five or ten years of experience with the affiliation, that it would be agreeable to all concerned if the treaty could be extended. Of course, this may not occur and the affiliated nation citizens or even the people of the U.S.A. may be very glad to see the end approach. However, if the affiliation is as successful as it might be envisioned, then certainly the question of mutually agreeable extension will come up as the treaty nears its termination.

However, as previously noted, the last ten years of the treaty are not going to be as nice as the first ten years. If the renegotiations wait until there are only a few years more to go, the investors will already have started cutting back on their investment and maintenance, unemployment will be rising and there will be angry strikes, agitation, and other unfriendly occurrences. The insiders who are making plans to seize military control of the newly disaffiliated nation will be willing to invest considerable funds and effort to make sure there is no extension.

Thus if a mutually agreeable extension is going to happen, it would have to happen before the situation starts to deteriorate. For this reason, it would be wise to set a time limit for such an extension agreement. The agreement should be negotiated and signed before the halfway point is reached; that is, in the first ten years of the affiliation.

The extension might provide some different terms. If so, these terms would not take effect until the end of the original twenty year term. Therefore if anyone felt that his interest was adversely affected by the negotiated revisions, he could have plenty of time to rearrange his affairs before the new rules could take effect.

Thus if mutual agreement were achieved, the union could be extended for another ten years, for a total term of thirty years. At the end of the original twenty years, there could be another opportunity to extend it again, with new modifications that, again, would not take place until ten years from the time they are negotiated.

In this manner the union could be extended as long as both parties desired, and under whatever terms were mutually agreeable. From the viewpoint of the investor, he will be quite safe. He has just as much warning of unfavorable changes in rules as he has of disaffiliation if such should occur. He can sell out, or cut back on investment, whatever he decides is best without any time pressure or necessity to sell under temporarily adverse conditions.

The potential expropiator must make his moves ten years in advance of the time when he could hope to actually seize power. He has to convince the people that disaffiliation is desirable at a time when they have had enough experience to personally know the advantages and disadvantages. If things are going bad, he will win. If things are going good, he will probably lose out in his bid for power. Even if he succeeds in getting the people to vote for disaffiliation, he cannot be sure that he will retain his leadership for another ten years. It may be that he does the dirty work and someone else reaps the rewards.

All of the details, the symbols, the languages, the customs, the differential in skills and education, the tastes, the attitudes, all of these are surmountable. It would take a lot of effort, but there is ample precedent to guide the way. Incidentally, once we start taking the multilingual requirements seriously, we will have much more success in developed as well as in underdeveloped countries. We may also see a considerable improvement in the morale of our own Spanish speaking neighborhoods when increased importance is accorded to non-English language and cultural values.

XI

DO SOMETHING!

If you are concerned about an issue such as inflation, or crime, or unemployment, you may want to do something besides read about it. You may want to take some direct action.

Congress makes the laws and in the end, congressmen will decide what will be done, if anything. But congressmen by long experience have learned to delay action until they are absolutely sure what it is that the people really want them to do. Most issues have supporters pushing in opposite directions. Congressmen avoid such issues since they fear, with good reason, that no matter which side they take, they will lose votes in the next election.

This seems strange until you think about it for awhile. But it isn't strange at all. Suppose a congressman takes a position on a controversial issue where his people are split 50-50. Those who strongly oppose his position will remember his "wrong" vote and will try to punish him in the next election. Those who support his position may very well consider it quite routine, "He is just doing what any reasonable man would do." So their support is lukewarm. Maybe the next issue finds them strongly opposing their congressman's position and deciding to punish him for his vote on that issue.

Thus any congressman must stick to non-controversial issues if at all possible. If he is forced to take a clear position on a controversial issue, he wants to be very sure that he picks the right side. The right side has little to do with the actual merits of the issue, or even how the congressman himself may feel about it. The right side is the side favored by a large majority of the people in his voting district.

Thus your problem is very simple. You must convince the congressman that it will be safer to support your proposal than to avoid or oppose it.

It is easy for him to support non-specific proposals. He loses no votes that way. You need to write only one letter if you are to be satisfied with such non-action action. He will send you copies of his speeches deploring crime, or describing his concern about inflation, etc., and he will tell you that he voted to create a committee to study the problem. But this is all wasted effort.

In order to get action on a specific proposal, you must convince him that he has to take action if he wants to be sure of surviving the next election. Your congressman must receive an avalanche of mail supporting your specific proposal.

Let us assume that you would like him to propose a bill enacting one specific proposal, perhaps one that is described in this book. Let's say that you are willing to invest a little time and money into such a project. Your first objective should be to get twenty other people to write to your congressman asking him to act on the particular proposal that you favor.

One way to do this is to persuade twenty of your friends that the idea is really worthwhile enough for them to write a letter. Another way is to use this book to persuade them for you. You could buy extra copies at a discount, mark each copy to direct attention to the particular proposal that you favor, and give them to your friends with the understanding that if they agree with the proposal, they will write a letter to your congressman urging his support. You could also send a copy of the book, marked the same way, to your congressman and let him read it in detail. Perhaps some of your friends will be inspired by your example and maybe they will buy additional books to give to their friends, etc. Your congressman may find himself flooded by letters and marked books. If you cannot afford the expense of purchasing extra copies of this book, you have herewith the author's permission to copy portions of this book for such purposes provided that the title and author's name are also included for reference.

The key strategy is to get many people to concentrate on just one issue at a time. If the congressman sees that this is a potentially important issue, he will first try to find out what the other people in his district think about it. Thus your first milestone of success is when your congressman includes your proposal in his newsletter and asks his constituents what they think about the idea.

If the response to this poll is hostile or inconclusive, then the congressman will do his best to avoid the issue. He really doesn't want to get involved. But if the people respond favorably, then he will start making speeches and proposing legislation, reporting his efforts with great pride to the people back home. In a short period of time, he may even convince you that it was his idea in the first place . . .

Don't rely on it! Keep up the pressure until the proposal becomes law and you see its effects taking place. If you and your friends lose interest, your congressman will also lose interest. There are always other issues that are competing for his attention, and he has to decide which issues are safe to neglect. You must keep him convinced that your issue is one he must continue to support. If you can keep the pressure on, you will probably see some sort of useful results in the end. If you let up, someone else will be convincing him that the most important thing is to get some new government contracts or build some more roads in his district.

Sometimes there is a snowball effect where other congressmen see some possibilities for gaining favor by supporting the same or similar proposals. If their people also respond with enthusiasm, then the proposal will receive prompt attention. As soon as a majority of congressmen see the issue as a safe vehicle for gaining prestige with their voters, prompt enactment is certain.

This is the way our democracy works. Our congressmen are in fact as well as in name the servants of the people. However the system doesn't work unless there is a definite campaign to enact a specific proposal. So, if you want to do something, here is your opportunity.